Copyright © 2018 by Dr. Anne Watson,
with a contribution by Nicole Henderson

All rights reserved. No part of this book may be reproduced or used in any manner without written permission of the copyright owners except for the use of quotations in a book review.

First issued in paperback, ebook and audio in October 2018.

The image on the cover is of a painting by Dr. Anne Watson.

ISBN 978-1-77256-174-6 (paperback).
ISBN 978-1-77256-175-3 (eBook).
ISBN 978-1-77256-176-0 (Regular CDs).
ISBN 978-1-77256-177-7 (MP3 CD).
ISBN 978-1-77256-178-4 (Digital Download).

Inquiries regarding requests to reprint all or part of *FLASH!: The Science Behind Intuition* should be addressed to Envision Books. To order directly from the publishers, please call toll-free (North America) 1-888-885-8616, or order online at www.envision-books.com. Any other inquiries can be directed by mail to: Envision Books, Suite 274—7655 Edmonds St, Burnaby British Columbia, V3N 0C3.

Envision Books
an imprint of Post Hypnotic Press Inc.

FLASH!
THE SCIENCE BEHIND INTUITION

by Dr. Anne Watson,

With Contribution by Nicole Henderson

2018

Envision Books

"Intuition is faster, smarter, and more benevolent than reason."
Dr. Anne Watson, 2016

FLASH!
THE SCIENCE BEHIND INTUITION

by Dr. Anne Watson,

With Contribution by Nicole Henderson

2018

Envision Books

CONTENTS

Preface iii

PART I: KNOCK KNOCK, WHO'S THERE? 1

Chapter One: Helping Us, One Intuition At A Time...3

PART II—WHEN VISIONS ARE BESTOWED 13

Chapter Two: A Vision Appears 15

Chapter 3: What The Puzzle Was 19

Chapter 4: The Message 27

Chapter 5: Good Company 31

PART III: THE SCIENCE 41

Chapter 6: How Do We Receive Messages From Light?...43

Chapter 7: Above And Below, In And Out 51

Chapter 8: There it is! PREAFFERENCE 63

Chapter 9: An Inborn Will To Harmony 69

PART IV: ACCESSING AND USING INTUITION 73

Chapter 10: Remote Viewing and Healing 75

Chapter 11: When Intuition Can't Be Accessed..107

Chapter 12: Fast Track To Alpha and Intuition Using EEG..117

ENDNOTES..125

APPENDIX..133

Preface

EVERYONE HAS INTUITIONS. The instant we know something without knowing how we know it, without conscious reasoning, we are having an intuition. Often it's a gut feeling that keeps us safe. Sometimes it's an inspired solution to a baffling problem which hits us like a light bulb going off in our heads: flash! It could be a vision, a dream, or even a compelling message spoken by an unseen visitor. Occasionally, if it is a warning, we get a sudden constriction of the heart muscles. Alternatively, if it is a good thing, we can feel inexplicably joyful and *right* with the world. Intuition is, as author Simone Wright says, our first intelligence. She even named her latest book about it *First Intelligence.*[1]

We all have it, but we don't all call it the same thing. It goes by many names:

- The Universe
- Source (of All Knowledge)
- inner voice
- spirit guide
- sixth sense
- innate wisdom
- psychic knowledge
- instinct
- a hunch
- a premonition
- the unconscious now being manifested
- the link between the conscious and the unconscious
- God

In 2004, when I began researching intuition, there were no books available on the science behind intuition, nothing that explained where intuitions come from, and how we physically receive and make sense of them. There were a few books on increasing your intuition, where there are now dozens of such books. There were a few internet articles, some of which were faith-based cyber pamphlets on the uses of intuition to get "closer" to a divine entity: the bloggers' God. The rest of the articles were about how to respect your intuition and how to increase access to it through meditation (and how to meditate) and a few about how to increase your psychic intuitive powers. Now, in 2017, there is a plethora of books examining, discussing and celebrating intuition (how to use it, how to increase it, how to "master" it, how to not ignore it), and there are even a few books and articles professing scientific explanations about how and why we receive intuitive information. A lot of these say "brain science shows us…[something]," but then fail to cite the brain science studies. Several articles do contribute to our knowledge of the science of intuition, but are *not* the science *behind* intuition. For example, one brain science study even proves that intuition exists, in case there are people who aren't convinced. Those results were published as *The Science of Intuition: How to measure 'Hunches' and 'Gut Feelings'*. The researchers flashed subliminal images designed to simulate intuitive information, and found the flashed participants did much better on their predictive task and got better at using their intuition.[2] So this was good science, but not a complete scientific disclosure of how intuition is formed, and gets to us, and adds to our lives.

As far as my most current readings reveal, all the titles promising the science behind intuition fall short of integrating scientific knowledge we have today linking DNA, holograms, wave genetics, the pineal gland, the heart, the gut, our skin, and the neuronal miracle of something called preafference and, of course, spirit guides. Simone Wright's *First Intelligence* comes closest to pulling all those threads together in a most readable way, but with some omissions across the scientific cognate disciplines which create and support the conditions for intuitions. Until now. This is the whole shebang.

FLASH! The Science Behind Intuition is the long-awaited round-up of where does it come from, and where does it go, and why do we have it?

This book had to wait for certain supporting evidence to be available, like MRI scans, innovations to EEG procedures, and the results of some DNA studies, in order to know what we know, but it is time to go public now, while interest in intuition is high.

When you read the science, it might increase your desire to access your intuition, because it will become clear that we are designed to do just that. At least 18 *complete* books about improving intuition have been published in the last few years. According to all of them, life gets better when we follow our intuition. (See Appendix A: Goodreads List of Books About Intuition). There are plenty of "how to" books out there for readers who wish to read on, to learn how to make their lives and this world a better place. Beyond "how to," *FLASH! The Science Behind Intuition* will inform you why you should improve your access.

When I started the intuition literature search, I looked for corroboration, scared to talk about what I knew about intuition, because I thought people would think I was crazy (intuition was not mainstream in 2004). You see, I had received a flash!—a vision, a powerful intuition, a brilliant insight, that was targeted specifically towards me. Early on, even when corroboration was hard to find, I stopped being scared when I started talking to people about my vision. Instead of derision, I found people wishing they could receive such visions. I became sure of what I was saying as I described my quest for substantiation. I also became sure that other people can have the same kind of access to intuition as I had been given.

As I have since found, when you intentionally seek and receive intuitions, you enter a world of sureness. You are comfortable with your decisions, resulting in far greater happiness than through relying on reasoning. Now, I am not just comfortable but brave, because I know the science, and I trust my unfailing intuitions. While it is wondrous, there is nothing crazy herein.

This is what intuition is:
Instinctive feelings or sensations "influencing" us.

It is knowing, without knowing how you know: it just comes to you, in a flash of insight.

Intuition is faster, smarter, and more benevolent than reason, allowing us to "make faster, more accurate, and confident decisions."[3]

Intuition is inspired knowledge, knowledge that comes from a place other than our own minds: a benevolent place.

If you want things to go smoothly in your life, you will access your intuition and follow it. Those who encourage others to go with the gut are among the happiest people (like Oprah Winfrey, Deepak Chopra, Gregg Braden, Eckhart Tolle, and Esther Hicks). Celebrities who follow their spirit guide recommend that you follow yours, so you can recognize *how* your choices, your ideas, your kindnesses, and your path can benefit from a greater wisdom than is available through reasoning alone.

The book begins with illustrative stories of people helped by intuition to overcome obstacles in their lives, which leads up to the story of how an inspired vision showed me where intuition actually comes from.

Not quite believing what I had been shown, or at least wanting proof, I looked into history to find out who else had received such a vision: some very well-known people, as it turns out. And all of them were compelled to tell about it.

So, tell I would. But, because I wanted to be accurate, I plunged into years of scientific detective work, finding out how so many people's similar visions came to be. I needed to know how do our bodies receive intuition and where does it go once we have received it?

The fields of Biology, Neuroscience, Wave Genetics, all the contributors were searched. New information from Quantum Physics, Sync, Precognition, and DNA studies got included here, and explained in lay terms. Complicated concepts like the extraordinary phenomenon of brain pathways which light up BEFORE the event or stimulus has appeared, these are examined in connection with intuition. (Some call these "presentiments," or "anomalous anticipatory activity,"[4] meaning the researchers agree this pre-knowledge cell-action occurs but is not-normal, whereas in fact these precognitions appear to be far from anomalous, and often work without our knowing about their presence, therefore are not always presentiments, but always present. The field is exploding with research results, some of which are hard for the researchers to explain.)

There is a contribution from Nicole Myers Henderson who uses her *intuition* to perform remote viewing, seeing into the perceptions of distant others for healing purposes. She gives an explanation into the science of intuitive remote viewing.

There is a description of what happens when people cannot access their intuition.

Finally, there is description of how to use visual brainwaves on a computer screen hooked into an EEG machine (electroencephalogram) to get in sync with another person's wavelengths, which is the quickest way for a novice to get into an Alpha state of mind, the best mind state for contacting your inner voice, the Universe.

After reading this book, you should be more inclined to trust your inner voice, because scientifically and spiritually, it is the right thing to choose for a harmonic life.

This book will show that by asking the Universe, and trusting it, you will find a kinder, better solution.

May this book light your way towards being guided by intuition.

Dr. Anne Watson

PART I
KNOCK KNOCK, WHO'S THERE?

Would you answer if someone came knocking with affirmations of love for you? Or just to help you? What if it was someone or something you couldn't actually see? Would you let them in?

Chapter One:

Helping Us, One Intuition At A Time

In 1997, when I first heard my spirit voice, it was so loud, I looked around searching for whoever was in the empty room with me. No one! But the deep voice started by saying, "You are beloved." That got me crying, because at that time I did not feel beloved at all. The voice had more to say, in its authoritative, but friendly tone. "Do not stay where you don't feel loved." "To love and be loved is all," and then a suggestion to "Pass all your ideas, wishes, dreams, thoughts, decisions through ME."

Although not religious, I was convinced this was probably what others call "God" speaking directly to me at a time of great emotional crisis when my marriage was disintegrating. The comfort of this disembodied voice was immediate and immense. I felt loved in the world. My actions were sure now. I was instructed to go forth and find love and follow my passions. I have been doing that ever since, and I have never been happier in my whole life. I have many friends and a rich and varied life. I feel so loved, and I look it.

Best of all, any time I want to talk with that voice, I simply have to get into peace, what I now know to be an Alpha wavelength mind-state. Then I close my eyes, make contact (the voice always immediately responds with how much I am loved) and then I ask my question(s). I have come to know the difference between the Universe answering me, or alternatively, my own reasonable thoughts or answers (but not inspired ones): the intuitive answers come tumbling down on top of the question. I don't even get the question out before the answer is spoken. For example, I might ask for guidance in how to say something difficult to a friend, to get the issue on the table without hurting their feelings. I will make contact right now, as I write, regarding my soon-come job as Master of Ceremonies at a friend's wedding. I don't want to do it, for I fear it will be a lot of work and has the possibility of overtaking the mood of the wedding, because I am a big presence. So I just asked the Universe for help and it said "We are with you on this. Keep every announcement under three minutes, so you will not dominate but just move the proceedings along." There, with that guideline I have been given parameters which reduce the workload for me, and prevent "MC mic overload." I love the Universe! It is so much smarter than I.

Friends have benefited, too, when I access my inner voice for them, at their request. "Give me a moment," I say. I close my eyes and get into a calm, alert and focused state and ask the Universe their question. One friend wanted to know why his marriage was breaking up. The answer was "the book." This carried no meaning for me, but when I said it aloud he paled, "Oh, it's cos I read her diary, and I shouldn't have. She wrote about a female lover. That's why she said she couldn't trust me any more. I read her diary." The Universe said the trust issue was more hers than his.

Since the answers are always smarter than us, my friends are impressed. Some want to be able to access their own inner wisdom. They want to be sure of their decisions, of their path. They want their conversations to be informed but kind. These friends all know what it feels like to access their intuition randomly. They each have had at least one experience in their lives where listening to an inner voice *changed* their lives. These are their encounters:

Encounter 1: *Divine Intervention*
By Kate Kelly

I BELIEVE IN DIVINE INTERVENTION simply because it happened to me, well, me and my three children. It was early Saturday morning and I was taking my six year old daughter, Shannon, to dance class. My husband was away for the weekend and so I had my other two children with me four year old son, Connor and my one year old son, Quinn. All three children were safely in their car seats, snug in the back of our small Honda Civic. It is always a great deal of work getting the children ready to go anywhere so I started early: boots, jackets, hats, sippy cups, bottles, teddy bears and Batman figures and everything else we might need. The process went quicker than expected with minimal bumping and crying, and lo and behold I was early for Shannon's class.

The three children were quiet and drowsy from the car ride and so I decided to drive around, enjoying the peace and sipping on my coffee while the kids slept undisturbed in the back. I enjoy driving and the car was a standard four on the floor with quick pick up and a lot of fun to wheel around. I drive quickly. I am a very good driver but not a very patient one. Consequently, I never usually stop fully and count to three at a stop sign, or wait for anything when the light turns green. So the car was a soft haven, the children blissfully asleep and me joyful in the moment which felt totally mine for the first time in quite a while. I was touring around the back roads of subdivisions where there was very little traffic and I was lost in unexpected tranquility until I realized I would have to start heading back to the dance studio.

I was on Grandview St., south of King St., which is also Highway 2, running east and west right through Oshawa.

I came to the intersection and my light was red for a long time, accommodating the King St. traffic. Ironically, after so much time to spare, I was beginning to get anxious about making it to the dance studio on time. My left hand was on the steering wheel and my right hand was on the gear shift, ready to pull into the intersection as soon as the light turned green, and speed my way back through town. As my mind was racing with my thoughts and watching the traffic and glancing at the lights and at the children in the rear view mirror and the myriad of things the mind processes at such a time, I heard a voice saying "Wait… wait… wait." I sat back in my seat, listening, and waiting and not even wondering, just waiting as I had been instructed to do.

The light turned green and still I sat there, kind of in wonder, waiting for I didn't know what, when a Ford truck came barreling through the intersection. I watched the truck speeding through the red light, the driver's head was down, as if he had dropped something on the floor of the cab and was looking for it, oblivious to the light he was running or to anything that would have been in his way… anything like a small Honda Civic with a mother and three children. In moments the truck was through the intersection and again I heard the voice, "Ok, now you can go." I put the car in gear and drove into the middle of the intersection where only moments ago the speeding truck had been.

I don't know if I actually said 'thank you' out loud, but a very deep sense of gratitude came over me, and I felt like crying for the lives of myself and my children spared by something I cannot describe other than as divine intervention.

Perhaps this is where the idea of the guardian angel comes from, some greater power or intelligence that intervenes at times and stops something that is obviously going to happen, from happening. Or perhaps it is just our own untapped abilities, our own universal intelligence, our own precognition or our own ability to be all things at all times, characteristics of our own *beingness* that we have yet to acknowledge or even be able to understand. For now, I am calling it divine intervention and I am happy with that definition because we humans, we mere mortals, are all of the Divine.

Kate Kelly is a musician and author in Peterborough, Ontario, who recently learned how to access the mindful state prerequisite to talk to one's own spirit guide. She is now practicing the very things recommended in this book, and is able to directly receive her own insights *anytime* she asks. Her children are safely grown and gone from the home. It took her a long time until now (some 20 years) to reliably say, "Give me a moment" and receive intuition from Source for her own tricky questions. She practices mindfulness and meditation.

The next friend, Christine, would describe herself as a life-long spiritual person who immediately began accessing personal intuition on demand after having the following encounter which made her forever open to instinct beyond reason.

Encounter 2—*Hair-Raising Highway*

By Christine Carleton

1962. AS A TEENAGER IN HIGH SCHOOL I was out with a bunch of guys. With nothing special to do, five guys and I piled into a small white Vauxhall with a blue stripe. We decided to head south of the city to the Edmonton International airport for coffee. It was a quiet, dark evening as fog engulfed the highway. We were kibbitzing as teens do, when I got a sense there was something on the highway up ahead.

The 'Calgary Trail' was a six-lane, divided highway with little traffic that evening. I said "Hey Ken, I think there is something on the highway, get into the middle or outside lane." Ken resisted. "Christine, it's foggy, there is nothing out there. No one is on the road." I was being a front seat driver, which was not going any place fast. The other guys started to tease me. "What's this? Female intuition? Are you nuts? There's no one out tonight! It looks like we are the only ones on the highway."

I took the ribbing, and joked with them, but insisted there was something ahead. We were bombing along at about 70+ mph (113 + kph) and the miles were rapidly passing by. Again, I asked Ken to move over to the centre lane. Again, resistance, fully supported by the other fellows. I continued to pester them. Then my voice became insistent, commanding, in a way not often heard within teen social groups.

One of the fellows in the back seat, asked me to 'settle-down'. He asked Ken to appease me, and move into the centre lane. Just as the car was moving to the left, our headlights caught the shadow of a car stopped in the first lane, plus the silhouettes of a couple of people standing in the second (middle) lane beside that vehicle. We missed them, we missed them, by a hair's breadth.

Everyone in the car saw those folks standing on the highway. Everyone was stunned. Questions followed. "What the heck are those people doing standing in the middle of the highway on a dark foggy night?" More importantly, "Christine, how did you know?"

I didn't know, I just felt something blocking on the highway ahead.

It kind of spooked a couple of the guys. There was a lot of silence and reflection over coffee. I always listen to my messages from light, to my intuition.

Christine Carleton is currently an aromatherapy specialist in Vancouver. She reads avidly in the areas of harmonic frequency affecting the brain, and DNA modification, especially as affected by smell. She has led many people into spirituality with her insights and kindness.

Christine has always presented in the calm, mindful state that is associated with accessing intuition. Not so, Annemarie, a Dutch surfer girl with bubbling energy.

Encounter 3—*Narrow Escape*

by Annemarie Holwerda

A FEW YEARS AGO I was at a party at a beach town in Costa Rica. It was late and almost everybody had left: the only ones still there were completely drunk and high people, so I decided, time to go home.

I left the party with a Tico (Costa Rican) boy who was also very drunk and high. Myself, I'd had a couple too many to drink, but was still okay.

We were staying in the next town. Everybody always hitch-hikes from the one town to the other, never a problem. Also, being with a boy at night, probably no problems because of that, too.

A car stopped. Four or five guys were in the back of this big car. The Tico boy got in the car looking and thinking of nothing and happy to have a ride. I was ready to get in, until I saw an older middle aged white guy in the crowd of mainly younger guys. I saw his face and it looked very nargly. It changed and became a monster in my head. (Note: I was not taking any drugs.)

Then my mind flashed back a few seconds to where that same face had been grabbing the Tico boy's arm and whispering something in his ear. I could not hear him but something told me he had said, "Yeah, we want the girl to get in."

I knew what the monster had said without even hearing what he had said. I just knew.

Alarm bells started going off in my head; I heard "Get Out Now!!" from inside my head.

I got out as fast as I could. Grabbing the Tico boy's arm, I was begging him to come with me. He, at first. completely did not understand, but he did get out with me. We both got out, and luckily another car past, so the big car drove off.

We hitched another ride, with nice kind people. My Tico friend started to remember what the old guy had said to him in Spanish (which at that time I did not understand). It was something like, "You get the f*%# out, you....*#$#* we want the girl to get in." And he had given the boy a hard pinch on the arm, which I hadn't seen.

I always thought I had a good intuition about these things, and was so happy I had one that night. Maybe it was my clearest message from light, ever.

Annemarie Holwerda is a surfer who has spent most of her 20's away from her native Holland, catching waves along the Panama—Costa Rican coast. She listens to her voices from light but does not get them often. She would like to.

The next and final story is about the inner voice being the guide of a woman's life. Sometimes intuitions arrive in a sudden flash, while other times a series of lights going on is a better way to describe the benevolent interventions of intuition.

Encounter 3—*Journey From There To Here*

By Marianne Helsby

THE JOURNEY FROM WARRINGTON, UK (where I was born) to Vancouver, Canada (where I belong) is a long one: about 4530 miles or, in my life, about 55 years.

In the first 12 years of my life, I got halfway there, as my family wandered with my father's jobs from UK through Africa, Iran, and New Zealand before finally settling in Canada, near Toronto, Ontario. It was not MY own messages from light being followed by my family bringing me along, but theirs.

The journey was then delayed about 45 years, during which time I did all the "right" things. I got educated, married, divorced, had a son, worked a long time for a mental health facility in the isolation of Ontario's far north, got more education and, sadly, attended the death of my mother. The "right" things weren't always giving me happiness. I tried moving to Toronto.

Shortly after moving there, the phone rang at my small apartment beside Lake Ontario. At that time, as the social worker Director of a Young Offender home (an open custody prison for young people guilty of minor offences), I was enjoying my job's challenges, but it was sucking the life out of me with insatiable problems. Plus, after hours, I was deep into group work with women who had multiple personalities, for whom I acted as a therapist. In researching their Dissociative Identity Disorder, I saw how each personality had an 'observing self' that remained neutral and peaceful and was aware of all of these other personalities. It was as if they each had the near possibility of accessing intuition which might help them appease their other selves. I enjoyed those women.

However, in the harried life of downtown Toronto, I was mentally and emotionally exhausted—and my soul had evidently sent out a strong demand for change. Out of the blue, a woman named Nancy called, asking me if I would consider coming to work in Vancouver, in a women's prison. Her voice was compelling but what did I know about a women's prison? I was a social worker, yes, but had never done a practicum in such a setting. This group home where I was working now was in the Corrections field, sure, but a women's prison! Those would be career criminals, surely? Would I like working with tough cases? While my mind was saying, "hm…not so sure about that…," my mouth was saying, "Love to."

An 'inner guide' just set me on the last leg of the journey from there to here. What surprised me was that all mental confusion immediately cleared. Relief and happiness replaced anxiety, and all I had to do was pack and leave.

The 'rightness' of my journey was affirmed every day, across 5 provinces. Here I was heading west at the ripe old age of 55 years, realizing this was my dream finally coming true, and with no effort on my part!

I hadn't given any thought to where I would live. When I reached BC, I got out of the car to sit on the side of a mountain overlooking a huge lake. As I sat musing about where I should live, I looked down to see I was holding a large white rock in my hand. It was so nice. I decided to keep it. It felt right.

A friend introduced me to what immediately became my new home—a village by the sea with a magnificent beach. It was affirmed in my heart how much I had been guided and helped on this journey to here, as I stood on the pier in my pretty village, and gazed toward the shore at the huge white rock there, the rock that symbolized my new home where my intuition had taken me—White Rock, B.C.

Marianne Helsby is a recently retired Vancouver Social Worker who regularly consults her inner voice to ensure she is receiving and following her messages from light. She is sought by many for her spiritual knowledge, especially around her meditation workshops and rebirthings.

When I asked these friends, and other friends, from intuition novice to expert, none of them knew where intuition came from. When I told them of my vision, they found the information most illuminating.

PART II—WHEN VISIONS ARE BESTOWED

I KNOW PEOPLE WHO MAKE FUN OF VISIONS and find it ridiculous that someone such as I, with a Doctorate, should give any credence to such "woo woo" concepts. I say, "Who are we to be surprised by anything in heaven and earth?" So they think I am religious. No. But my mind is open. Those with open minds will "get" this.

This painting was inspired by my vision - see the color version on the front cover.

Chapter Two:

A Vision Appears

IN 2004, A VISION CAME TO ME, unannounced, one fine (non-teaching) day in Ontario, Canada. It looked a lot like this, but much more vibrant and 3D.

Like psychedelic striped wallpaper materializing before my eyes, there suddenly appeared vertical columns with pulsating lights shimmering up and down inside them. Each thin tube was thrumming to its own sound, to the rhythm of its own oscillations. Side by side, the vibrating columns collectively formed a wide, wondrous pilaster of constantly shifting, harmonious light and sound. Brilliant light! Ecstatic music! It was right there, on my bedroom wall, that sunny July morning.

Ignoring my partner sitting beside me, I asked the wall, "What is this? What is this for?" and instantly, even as I framed my questions, a stranger's voice inside my head responded:

> "These are the messages we send. Those who are open to receiving them can be aware of them even as they are transmitted. The messages enter while you sleep, while you meditate, and occasionally while you are wide awake. They guide and enlighten you as to the ways of the Universe. They are the pre-knowledge your brain must have in order to function smoothly."

The pre-knowledge?

Who was saying this? This voice was not the nagging voice of my conscience, but a deeper tone. It was a man's voice explaining to me what I was looking at. In a flash of insight, suddenly I understood how the brain knows in advance which cells to excite and which to inhibit along an intended neural pathway. That is, which neurons the brain should engage and which it should avoid when we have an idea, a thought, or send a command to our bodies like, "pick up the cup," or "shout, he can't hear you," or "better look into what that banging noise is downstairs," or "The square root of 9 is…? 3": problem solving and behavior commands. The brain carries out such messaging for us so that we can function.

But in that flash of insight, I got it! Our brains receive messages for us, directives, commands, suggestions: messages sent through light.

Vibrating, oscillating light messages, shown in a vision to me, made me suddenly understand how the brain pre-knows. It's because the messages prepare it for what is to come, and these messages come to us from light.

Neuroscience illuminated—literally!

Messages from light arrive in our brains to prepare us to attend to what is coming up next in our minds.

Messages are sent to us, via light, to plan our next thoughts, ideas, movements, responses, reactions. Messages form consciousness.

Like a light bulb going off in my head, the stranger's revelation explained things about the brain over which I had been puzzling.

"Why are you showing me this?" I asked, out loud.

The deep voice continued,

"It is up to you to tell about it, because you know how the brain works and you can write in lay terms."

Okay, years ago, I co-authored a book about going to court and the law, so that children would be able to understand what was expected of them if they had to undergo the courtroom ordeal. The book became a best seller in Canada, the impetus for a court-orienting job that is now managed by what we call "Victims' Assistance Workers." Before we had these workers in police stations, standing by to mitigate victims' trauma, the book I co-authored with a Special Prosecutor in Child Sexual Assault cases (*So, You Have to Go To Court!*, 1986) became the gold standard for court preparation of young witnesses. Yes, writing for lay readers is something I can do. The visitor was right about that. But did I really know enough about the brain to write about it?

In my work as a Special Educator, I avidly read books on the brain, all sorts of articles about neuroscience, but I didn't claim to know how the whole brain works, just the parts that glitch for those with Learning Disabilities. I guess the stranger thought I knew enough to convey his message.

"Why?" I continued. What I meant was, why this was important? He understood what I was asking.

"For harmony. We emanate harmony frequencies."

At this point my questions were being answered so quickly it was difficult to determine which of us was asking and which one was answering.

"When all things go as pre-ordained, we enter a state of rightness, perfection—a state of harmony."

"Yes."

That was it. That was the whole exchange: end of vision, end of message. I got up and touched the wall, but there was nothing there now except wallpaper. All was back to normal, but everything had changed. It was the beginning of a profound journey for me into history, science, neuroscience, quantum physics, and mysticism, all of which are linked to intuition.

Chapter 3

What The Puzzle Was

APPARENTLY, GREAT VISIONS ARE frequently preceded by great puzzles.

I started puzzling a strange brain phenomenon (which I now call brain pre-knowledge) while doing "CSI of the brain." That's the diagnostic work I did as a Psycho-educational Consultant, finding out what might be causing learning problems. I did this work with all ages from K-12th grade, mostly in public schools, occasionally in private and faith-based schools, and sometimes in students' homes. In short, wherever people asked me to help them figure out why a student presented as more intelligent than their failing grades would suggest. I would show up with my battery of tests (some call it "assault with battery" but I made it fun). The tests have games and blocks and sentences and a little math, and are designed to show different aspects of brain abilities. The test results are far less interesting than watching students' processing as they complete the tasks. Referred students would be brought into a private space where I would figure out which parts of the brain were firing up well (learning strengths) and which parts misfired (weaknesses, called "Learning Disabilities" or LD). In these testing sessions, there were always things that made me wonder "Does the brain *know* what we are going to do before *we* know? If so, how can it?" You see, when I watched students work on problems, I saw evidence of what can only be "pre-knowledge." The brain seemed prepared for what was to come. It knew!

Again and again, I observed students as they sat with me, and I could see when a student had the correct answer but failed to give it.

For example, Kayla, a third grader, whom I watched prepare to say a correct answer. Unbeknownst to *her*, her brain replaced her chosen word, the answer she had thought of, with what her eyes saw without really looking. In this example, she was going to say "15"—it was on the tip of her tongue—but instead she said "jungle." The answer she planned to say got derailed and overridden by a stronger visual recognition impulse of suddenly noticing the jungle print on my blouse.

At that moment, Kayla could be the poster girl for THE PUZZLE.

The puzzle is NOT how, without any conscious plan, could a jungle-print blouse cause Kayla to speak aloud an unplanned word. No, skip-jump word replacements happen a lot with word finding problems. The neurons on the word retrieval path are not firing up properly. If brain cells (neurons) always behaved the way we wanted them to, we wouldn't do things like fall off our bikes, miss the bus, or say things we don't intend to say. We all make slips-of-the-tongue. Neurons—brain cells—pass information along so all the parts of an idea are picked up along the way. Slips-of-the-tongue and word-finding problems happen when planned information gets derailed along the neuronal pathway.

The neuronal path is like a train track along which brain cells pass information from one (station), one cell, to the next, until all information required to think or act in a certain way has embarked. By staying on track, the neurons avoid including wrong information from nearby cells.

Neuronal trains derail all the time, though.

Many things can derail a neuronal train, the train being the electrical routing causing messages to move from one neuron to another. You need the right chemicals in the brain to kick in at the right time to allow the neuronal train smooth passage towards the planned action. Sometimes chemicals or neurons just don't kick in properly.

I could easily explain all that to Kayla, after all, she is intelligent despite having Language Learning Disabilities (LD) in the association areas of the brain where words are stored: unplanned associations replace desired ones, or words just simply go missing. Kayla saying "jungle" instead of "15" was not a puzzle to me. Kayla's neurochemicals were off balance, as happens too often in a stressed young life. With less stress, good nutrition, exercise, sleep—all the best ingredients for a healthy body and brain—Kayla would make fewer errors and be better able to correct the ones she does make, although her LD brain wiring is such that the errors would never completely disappear.

For decades, it had been my work to help students anticipate and overcome these sorts of neuronal train derailings, glitches between thought and performance.

Because I read about the brain, I am able to show students what is causing wrong answers, ie. the neuronal train derailing, and not a lack of intelligence. Some cry or speak their relief to know that they are not "stupid" (that's how LD students feel, and how they are sometimes described by others, including some parents).

No, it was no puzzle to me that plans got unintentionally derailed, because that is commonplace for all of us, just more noticeably frequent for LD sufferers, who now learn that their constant derailings mean they have to work harder and double check to ensure everything is what they planned. Still, they are always thankful to know they are not "stupid."

No, for me the puzzle was not that neural plans sometimes glitched—entrainment accidents do happen—but rather HOW had the brain known the *right* neural pathway, a truth made obvious now by the student's visible preparation to take the right path but instead accidentally taking the wrong path? Kayla had already started showing me fifteen counters as soon as I posed the math question to her, as if she already planned her response. But her plan went wrong.

You see, when a plan goes *right*, all goes well. When a plan goes wrong, glitches occur (errors, miscues, mistakes, responses that baffle). The plan gets derailed. But that means *there was a plan!* A right plan: a path for the neurons to connect that would have resulted in a successful response. Everything in Kayla's brain was lined up to say what she intended to say. All her neurons were aroused for the successful uttering of "15". If she had spoken that answer, an answer I could tell that she knew, all would be fine. Instead, out came the nonsense, "JUNGLE."

These mistakes are always glitches between a planned smooth neural entrainment versus a wrong neural path. But HOW does the brain set out the correct path before we even choose the items that should rightfully follow the path? That path was ready for 15. Ready for it. Puzzle *that*.

Think. If a glitch derails the plan, then it follows that the brain knows in advance what we are going to do, and lays out the neural pathways for it. We discover the plan only when the path is blocked or diverges: goes wrong. From the billions of connections between cells—synapses—billions of synapses that could be made, the brain lays out a path along just those few required to effectuate that plan: to carry it out. The brain stops the wrong ones, inhibits the unnecessary ones, the blah-blah, the spurious, the circular, the tangential, the dead-end ones, blocking them off. Meanwhile it stimulates the right neurons ready to fire up along the effective path. The brain plans for success. Imbalanced neurochemicals cause glitches, screwing up those plans.

In my diagnostic work, my CSI of the brain, so many times a plan-oops-glitch pattern was evident to me in children with Dyslexia and Language LD. So many times I puzzled this:

The brain knows in advance what is coming, and prepares to receive and/or give information according to this genesis, and if the information is received or given without any screw-ups, things go well. If misinformation, (miscuing, mistiming, misfiring) occurs, then the plan fails: wrong information is received and/or wrong responses are given. But, from this we know:

THE BRAIN HAS A PLAN!

Furthermore, its plan is formed before the information is selected, because only when the right information is selected does the plan succeed. The right information has to be ready to roll out before the plan does. The right information is there. The plan comes. If the neuronal train is working well, the plan is successful.

Looking again at Kayla's 15-oops-JUNGLE blooper:

If things go well, the brain's plan has been followed.

Success!

If things don't go well, the brain's plan has been thwarted.

Failure!

Therefore, the brain had a plan.

Classic LD is seen when a student KNOWS the correct answer, plans to give it, but instead gives an accidentally wrong response.

With Kayla, I could see this little girl understood the questions. I could see and sometimes hear her forming a correct response. But often, between her plan and her answer, her planned response got hijacked and she gave a wrong answer.

The neural train MUST pull into each station at the precise time it is expected, or it will jump back and forth trying to pick up the missed information, or simply get lost on a spur. Kayla didn't know her response was wrong. To make a correction, she needed feedback. I asked her, "So, the answer is jungle?" and I pointed to the fifteen. "Sheesh! Sometimes I go coco-loco," she laughed at the absurdity of her wrong answer.

The glitching happened to this little girl frequently. Little did she know that she wasn't coco-loco: something *switched up* her brain's answering plan.

Interestingly enough, according to new research (2003), if I had taken her hand prior to posing a question, I might have noticed a slight change in temperature at the point where her autonomic nervous system was recognizing that a stimulus (a question) was coming, and this heating up would happen about 2-3 seconds before I would actually pose a question to her. James Spottiswoode and E.C. May (in 2003) measured such *pre-presentation of stimuli* changes in skin conductance which they called "Prestimulus Response."[5] This is the kind science I have waited for to support what was revealed to me by my stranger. But back in the 1980's and 90's neither I, nor these researchers, had an explanation for precognition, and nobody was talking about it in the LD literature.

Brains change plans on all of us, adults and children alike. Who among you never recalls saying something like, "Now why did I say that?" or "Why did I do that?" These infrequent glitches tend not to wreck our lives. They may even make us more empathetic and forgiving when others glitch. However, when brain-plan changes occur so often that they undermine daily functioning, that's usually when an expert is consulted, like myself.

I have found there is always a reason for persistent glitching. Always. Usually, it's built-in Learning Disabilities (LD).

In fact, this "right-plan, wrong-answer" *is* LD. Tired brains, wrongly wired brains, under-the-weather brains, chemically imbalanced brains, drugs-assaulted brains, knocked-around brains, distracted brains, anxious brains, fearful brains, too-sad brains, and even too-happy brains like when people fall headlong in love or have a totally distracting obsession (ask us why we don't like Pokemon cards in schools), these are all prone to causing neuronal derailing, a falling off of the brain's planned processing routing.

I wanted to know how the brain knows what to plan. Where does it get its advance knowledge? THAT was the puzzle I was puzzling when my unseen visitor arrived in my room with his answer to my puzzle.

Chapter 4

The Message

Messages are sent to us through light, as I was told that splendid morning. These messages are our intuitions, to prepare our brains to activate in certain ways so that we behave in a manner which will make our lives go more smoothly. The messages, the intuitions, are benevolent, and if followed, lead to states of harmony. To obey these messages is to take the rightful path for our own lives.

We can achieve a state of harmony
if we listen to the messages that come to us from light
and trust and obey them.

That was the revelation for me that July morning. It's what I am supposed to tell others, to help you and others learn to listen to your own messages from light, your intuitions, so your lives will go more harmoniously.

Memory can be elusive, even immediately after an event. I wanted to recall every word, and to avoid building logical conclusions into the stranger's instructions, so as soon as the visit was over, I immediately wrote down everything I knew about it.

What did I know?

- I knew I had witnessed a communication system far greater than any I'd ever experienced before—earthlings just doesn't manufacture lights that bright, nor sounds so sustainedly harmonic.
- I knew that the shadowy stranger, whose outline sat in my left peripheral vision, was mystical. I've never met a commentator who knew my thoughts before I did and who could answer my questions even as I was still framing them. This stranger knew me in a deep way which strangers normally don't.
- I knew that what I saw on my wall was fantastic: an array beyond any art work I have ever seen, with a limitless range of colors (afterwards I was stunned to realize they were mostly indigo blues, purples—from the short wavelength end of the visible spectrum, which should have restricted the hue diversity, but did not). It was a spectacular show!
- I knew I was being honoured: singled out for a private screening of this exquisite sound and light show, I felt chosen. I was flattered.
- I knew it was exciting to receive an answer to the "brain foreknowledge" conundrum which had for a long time puzzled me in my work diagnosing Learning Disabilities.
- I knew the stranger was right. What he said fit every recorded foreknowledge of events over which people marvel and then write magazine articles about.
- I knew from hearing people say "I should have listened to my instincts" that messages are given to us and, when we override them, we mess up.
- I knew not to stop the scene before it was done, but just question and answer when it felt right to do so.
- I knew I felt honored, yes, but I also felt scared. Who would believe me? People would think I was crazy. Messages in light? Messages sent to us, for us, for each

of us, by light? Really? That seemed unbelievable, even to me, given how many billions of people are on this earth.
- I knew I had to check it out before I wrote about it. I simply didn't trust a stranger in my bedroom on a hot sunny morning, telling me what to write, and showing off a visual display to knock my socks off. It could easily have been my imagination. If I could find nothing to support it, then it probably *was* nothing. I don't do street drugs or hallucinogens, so I wasn't "tripping" (but what a *trip* it was). But was it true, this visit? Did it really happen? Did anyone else ever get such a visit?

For the next few years, I embarked on a voracious crusade to see what truth there was in all this. I yearned to find corroboration, because I felt privileged to be on the trail of an idea so simple, yet so profoundly illuminating and ultimately complex. I wanted this to be true, but I also was on the lookout for evidence that is was just my imagination. I knew that any evidence which runs counter to a theory, in effect, busts that theory. I kind of wanted to find counter-evidence, then I wouldn't have to make a fool of myself writing about something you can't see, like intuition. I wanted the stranger's message to be right, and at the same time I would have been relieved if it was wrong. This, in 2004, was just weird:

Through light (in light) the Universe emanates harmony frequencies containing messages for guiding our lives.

At first, I thought it odd (even during the show) to feel compelled to speak aloud as the scene unfolded; I am not in the habit of giving play-by-play descriptions of what some may call a daydream. But post-vision, the more I studied, the more I found out about others who've seen visions similar to this, the more I noticed that they all felt compelled to share their visions, aloud or in writing. No matter where I searched, I came up with cases just like mine, where a vision has arrived and the receiver has been instructed to tell the world. *Many* well-known historical figures and modern scientists have reported visions similar to mine, and were obliged to tell. The more I read on this search, the more I found I was in good company.

Chapter 5

Good Company

Loads of people have visions. According to Dr. Dennis Gersten in *Are You Getting Enlightened or Losing Your Mind?*[26], visions of deceased loved ones happen all the time to many people and are considered "normal" in some cultures. Similarly "seeing" God, angels, saints, or indescribable light is also common. Reportedly, about half the people in North America alone are estimated to have received at least one of the above kinds of visions.

However, visions accompanied by sudden problem-solving insights with instructions to copy things down or share that knowledge, these are much rarer. "Problem-solved, now-write-it-down" visions are flashes of insight rather than flashes of ecstasy or re-acquaintanceships with the dead. I call these rarer visions "directed visions."

Who has received this kind of vision, similar to mine?

Oddly enough, for a church-avoiding self-styled intellectual such as myself, I found several instances of directed visions in *The Bible*. One of the very first in recorded history was Moses (about 1570 BCE). He saw a cloudy pillar of light. He was given a message to give to his people—this message was, of course, the Ten Commandments. He was compelled to share the message, and share it he did on some now-famous tablets. Did he get this direction in response to some leadership problems he was puzzling? Was he having trouble with the behavior of his people? Considering the social times and the nature of the Commandments (e.g. "Thou shalt not kill" and "Thou shalt not bear false witness against thy neighbor"), my guess is yes, probably. He did get a message from light, and we can assume it dealt with difficulties facing anyone trying to manage a large group of people in uncertain, lawless times.

Besides Moses, others in the Bible have received messages from light, and messages clothed in bright light are still common among mystics.

Pythagoras (circa 600 BCE) was a mystic and a scholar, a guru who was himself trained by priests and mystics before establishing a commune-type school to search for wisdom through silent worship. He had many visions providing insights into problems he was puzzling. At his school (which enrolled women as well as men), he developed mathematical theorems, of which his most famous is used for measuring triangles, as you might recall from math class: "The square on the hypotenuse is equal to the sum of the squares on the other two sides." It was true then, and is still true, much to the chagrin of junior high school students in examinations. Still, it goes to how his mind thought everything could be reduced to number. He thought the world's energy might be expressed in mathematical terms (just like Einstein did, thousands of years later). He also studied music and astronomy and figured out how vibrating strings produce *harmonious* tones when the ratios of the lengths of the strings are whole numbers. He also claimed he had heard "the harmony of the music of the spheres."[7] Was that what I heard? That harmonic music...

Buddha (563-483 BCE) had a directed vision. While still known as Prince Siddhartha, he was trying to find a way to eliminate the problem of earthly suffering. To that end he was sitting under a fig tree, in the light of a full moon, meditating.

Suddenly, he experienced "Supreme Enlightenment." The basic Buddhist tenets were reveled to him, as well as his new name, Buddha. After this supreme experience he went about teaching the Four Noble Truths to counter human suffering, as per his enlightenment messages. His audiences thereafter described him as "radiating light."[8]

About 1100 years later, around 600 CE, another famous messenger, Muhammed, the founder of Islam, would break from business activities and go to a nearby mountain to meditate. In a cave there, according to self-report, a spirit in a bright light seemed to "grab him by the throat" and give him messages about there being only one god.[9] At the time, people worshipped a lot of different gods and many people made their living from selling icons of these gods: there was much competition among icon sellers and much religious confusion among the people. As per his directed vision, Muhammed started preaching monotheism and generated a following in his "One God" belief. Although his messages were not actually written down into the Qu'oran until about a hundred and fifty years later, many believe the Qu'oran contains exactly what was said to Muhammed. His life-altering experience, his directed vision, is another instance of sudden insight from light addressing a tricky problem; too many gods and goddesses on the religious scene at that time.

Then a nun, Hildegard of Bingen (1098-1179) was to become a revered medieval author, linguist, philosopher, naturalist, poet, visionary, composer, and pharmacologist. An amazing list of accomplishments which came to her after, in 1141, she saw "a burning light, as large and as high as a mountain, divided at its summit as if into many tongues."[10] She tried to stay silent about it for fear of being ridiculed (hey, Hildegard, I know that feeling), and became ill whenever she refused to speak of her visions. She then received a "vision of divine light" which said "You shall proclaim it as you have heard and seen it…"[11] This is what she saw and proclaimed:

"Man is a part of creation and the force of life and healing are also within this creation. The healing principle is hidden within each person and can be summoned by these healing powers."[12]

Hildegard's "illuminated" approach to healing (including to healing herself now) was to gauge her patients' *viridatus*, their greenness or vitality. She simply observed the viridatus in her patients to determine what they needed (e.g. more or less exercise, or food, or sex), prescribing a new regimen plus some cleansing herbs, pretty much the way modern naturopathy proceeds.[13] After her illumination, every lecture, every writing, every healing was guided by her new belief that all lives equally carry God's Divine energy, which is this viridatus. Imagine how revolutionary that was when the culturally predominant hierarchical church preached going through priests and higher ups to get to God's Divine energy.

Shortly after Hildegard, along came Julian of Norwich (1342-1413). Like Hildegard, Julian was a nun. She claimed a vision in which she actually saw God as an entity who foresees everything.[14] It was this characterizing God as "foreseeing wisdom" which made Julian's spirituality so different from her contemporaries', and made her sought after for her wisdom. When she shared her vision as directed, she changed people's view of God's powers.

Later, in 1619, Descartes' radical notion of the harmony of all sciences "as one," united as Universal Wisdom, came to him in dreams. Up until then, Descartes had been an adventurer, eschewing his trained career in law in favor of fighting in the wars of whatever country he happened to be in when they were having a war, until he had a night of "three visions" which caused a radical shift within him, and he thereafter set aside adventuring and began furthering philosophy, physics and mathematics. Perhaps he is best known for his most famous line, "I think, therefore I am." His separation of mind and body known as Cartesian Dualism has come into disrepute lately, for if mind and body are separate, how then do they interact?[15] But, perhaps Descartes' directed vision will be re-evaluated in the light of *my directed* vision and subsequent studies. Hear this:

"Before the mid-twentieth century, for a long time the dominant philosophical view of the mind was that put forward by René Descartes (1596-1650). According to Descartes, each of us consists of a material body subject to the normal laws of physics, and an immaterial mind, which is not. This dual nature gives Descartes' theory its name: Cartesian Dualism. Although immaterial, the mind causes actions of the body, through the brain, and perceptions are fed to the mind from the body. Descartes thought this interaction between mind and body takes place in the part of the brain we call the pineal gland. However, he didn't clarify how a completely non-physical mind could have a causal effect on the physical brain, or vice versa, and this was one of the problems that eventually led to dissatisfaction with his theory."[16]

The pineal gland's role in receiving messages from light is explored later in this book, including how the non-physical mind can affect the physical one. (see the next chapter: *How Messages From Light are Received*). Descartes' visions were not wrong.

Meanwhile, about a century later, Emanuel Swedenborg (1688-1722) experienced visions in which he received instruction to "reveal the spiritual meaning of the Bible." Under the guidance of this "vision visitor," Swedenborg wrote his book called *The Worship and Love of God*—the foundation for a religious sect whose followers still meet today—based on a received message of how *love is the universal spiritual path*. One can only *imagine* how well Swedenborg and John Lennon would get along if they had been able to meet. Again, it looks as if Swedenborg's vision also was not wrong. Today, we see how water behaves when sent love messages, versus hate messages (see the work of Dr. Masaru Emoto whose water crystals are beautiful or destroyed depending on which emotion they received, respectively.[17]) Since our brains and our hearts are about 73% water, parts of us are no doubt as susceptible to love messages as are Dr. Emoto's ice crystals. Swedenborg's message he received from God is further confirmed today by Applied Positive Psychology's findings regarding love, self-love, romantic love, and all loving feelings: "According to Harvard Psychiatrist Dr. George Vaillant we shouldn't underestimate the power of love, because it's the key to happiness."[18]

In England, poet and artist William Blake (1757-1827) described a typical vision of his as "Not a cloudy vapor or a nothing. It is organized and minutely articulated beyond all that the mortal perishing nature can produce."[19] (Archaic language aside, this sounds much like the vision I saw.) Through such visions Blake came to believe that creation followed a cosmic catastrophe, nowadays well known as the Big Bang Theory, but unheard of back then. During this cataclysm spiritual beings "fell into matter."[20] Blake criticized how people separated the sacred from the profane, believing instead that everything is holy and that all people have the responsibility to attend to the *energetic activity of the divine spirit*. This is very similar to my own visitor's admonition to pay attention to and try to get in harmony with the energy messages received from the Universe (from the divine spirit). For Blake, those messages were everywhere, in animate and inanimate objects. About 150 years later, in 1942, Blake's admonition to attend to the energetic activity of the divine spirit was echoed by the famous scientist Dr. Nikola Tesla who said:

> "If you want to find the secrets of the Universe, think in terms of energy. There is a frequency or **vibration** of energy that fills the Universe. This energy is not only beneficial,

but also essential to all living cells whether human, plant or animal."[21]

In 1900, Max Planck, the father of quantum mechanics, described his "flash of light in the darkness": literally a light revealing to him the concept of "action" as a *physical quantity* corresponding to energy, multiplied by time.[22] From this, Planck developed a mathematical constant to represent the discontinuous structure of energy (e.g. objects can be in one place, then in the next instant in another place, without passing through any intermediary point—the nonlocal nature of matter, or what we call *quantum physics*). Often, terms like "seeing the light" are used to describe sudden insights and unexpected solutions to problems. In Planck's case, he actually saw a flash of light in the darkness. A flash! Furthermore, this occurred at the moment he saw the action concept unfold. He received the Nobel Prize for his theory of the quantum, and this concept was used by Einstein in developing the Theory of Relativity.

In 1921, an Austrian scientist named Otto Loewi discovered the first neurotransmitter.[23] He had a vision in a dream to conduct an experiment with frogs' hearts, during which experiment he found the neurochemical we now call **acetylcholine**. This was a directed vision. He had to publish it. Had to.

More recently, other scientists have described a vision very similar to mine.

In 2003, Steven Strogatz reported receiving a vision illuminating intellectual problems he was contemplating. A leading mathematician and researcher in the field of chaos-and-complexity theory, author of *Sync, The Emerging Science of Spontaneous Order,* Strogatz's vision was of oscillators behaving uncannily like molecules in fluid, trillions of them, but with many colors of fluid—a rainbow of colors—a different one for each frequency of grouped oscillators.[24] This image is so very similar to mine: Strogatz saw multiple, individually colored fluid containers—I saw multiple, individually colored columns, or containers. Strogatz used his vision's information to create mathematical models of sync, of how oscillators spontaneously get in sync, or in "harmony," if you will. I am using mine to promote understanding of how our brains are primed to get in harmony with their messages—similar visions.

In September, 2003, Dr. Manjir Samanta-Laughton was contemplating the missing piece in what makes the cosmos work. A medical doctor and cosmologist, author of *Punk Science*,[25] Dr. Samanta-Laughton had a sudden vision where she saw an infinity of spinning orbs. (In my own vision, the light orbs were turning/spinning as they moved up and down the columns.) At that moment, she immediately knew and understood what had eluded her before—the Black Hole Principle: Black holes are not destructive, they are the source of creation for the universe. An infinite source of light is at the centre of each black hole. Energy emits from these black holes, sometimes as electrons and sometimes as bursts of light. (Einstein had said electromagnetic energy was "packets of light" which he called photons). Samanta-Laughton's infinity of spinning orbs created an image which solved her problem of what makes the cosmos work—light energy emerging from the centre of black holes—photons sending messages through light.

Strogatz, Samanta-Laughton and myself had visions differing only slightly from each other's, each vision giving its viewer precisely what was needed to solve his/her individual intellectual puzzle, each being a variation of some part of the others' message.

While it could be argued that each of us simply would have come to enlightenment if we had puzzled long enough, that argument can't account for each of us stating independently and spontaneously that it wasn't just an idea that came to us, but a *vision*. Furthermore, none of us has had a repeat vision, although we have solved other intellectual problems, but none so profound and novel.

There are many vision recipients who, like me, were puzzling tricky intellectual problems at the time of their vision, and found their vision(s) illuminated their problems. The vision recipients, in turn, passed along their "world-improving" knowledge that they received in their vision, usually by writing about it and sometimes by preaching or lecturing about it.

Most people who receive knowledge through a vision simply get on with the business of disseminating that knowledge (except for Hildegard, who made herself sick by not sharing). Me? I couldn't help but wonder, if we are sent messages in light, how do these messages enter our brains? Well, I was told: through light. Yes, but how does light take the message into our brains, into our thoughts?

This was a major question for me. If I couldn't find *how* messages enter our brains, how could I believe they did that? If light-messages are sent, how are they received? Corrobation for me, through good company, was not sufficient to induce me to try to publish these ideas. I needed independent, scientific proof that I was actually saying something other people, beside myself, would find fascinating and useful and, moreover, accurate. I dug deeper into the brain and the energy field in which we live.

PART III
THE SCIENCE

The more scientifically sophisticated the machinery to look inside the brain and body, the less scientific and the more spiritual we become.

Chapter 6

How Do We Receive Messages From Light?

WHILE I WAS RECEIVING the visitor's message, I knew that the lights, the vibrations, and the humming were not incidental; they all were vital to the message I was receiving, they all had something to do with how we get messages from light, including how I was currently getting the vision itself. What, inside me, was ready to receive messages from light?
I needed to find something that could take unwritten and unspoken messages from the energy field which our brain is tuned into, and turn them into usable information. Here is a quote from the physicist *Nassim Haramein*.[26]

> There's a fundamental field of information that is the source of our consciousness. Consciousness is not an epiphenomenon of your brain, it's actually something that your brain is tuned into like a radio is tuned into a set of information.

I am not a radio. I do not have antennae or dials. But something in me acts as if I was a wave receiver. Let's see what the candidates are for that function.

Obviously, my eyes receive information from light, because when I close them, I can't see: I cease getting the picture. But wait! If I closed my eyes while looking at the vision projected on my bedroom wall, I could still see it. Also, whenever I try to invite my intuition to come to me, I close my eyes for greater viewing success in case it plans to send me visuals to support its answers. So, I don't think messages come to us from light via our eyeballs, although some may.

Where, then?

When first I read about the pineal gland, located in the brain, I got excited. This gland is often called the third eye. Many believe the pineal gland to be the receptor site for non-sensory information. That is, information that comes to us not from our five senses. You may recall Descartes' belief that the Pineal gland was the interface between the mind and the brain, the mind dealing in non-sensory information. Non-sensory information comes to us from *insight, from intuition*. If you believe that some thoughts arrive through insight, or intuition, then they have to arrive in our minds somehow and the Pineal gland was the only thing I discovered to be up to the task. It is not, however, located on the surface of our brains, ready to receive light messages. It's situated deep inside the brain, parallel to the space between our eyebrows.

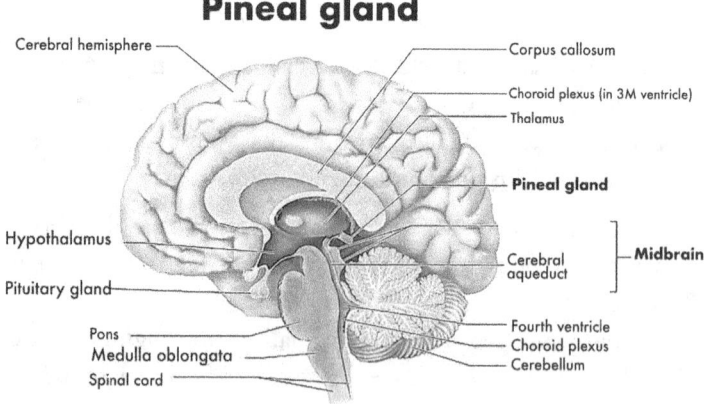

Illustration of the location of the pineal gland inside the brain, from https://en.wikipedia.org/wiki/Pineal_gland.

If we are having messages sent to us from light as energy, then within our bodies, something must be ready to receive the vibrations of the energy, the electromagnetic oscillations of it. It turns out that the pineal gland is ready-made for the job of built-in receiver of light messages. Even though they can't "see" light from their depths, pineal glands activate to light—they activate to increases in the energy vibrations within light. The electrical activity in the cells in pineal glands increases in the presence of increasingly rapid light impulses. Increasing pulsations from active electromagnetic oscillations create concomitant increases in the frequency of the pineal gland's energy oscillations—it gets excited, all fired up, when electromagnetic messages are arriving. As if that wasn't exciting enough to think about sender-receiver energy vibrations rising to match themselves up in their frequencies, to top it all off, we recently found out that **Dimethyltryptamine (DMT)** is manufactured in the Pineal gland.

"Dimethyltryptamine (DMT) is a [psychedelic] neurotransmitter which naturally occurs in many plants, and is found within the pineal gland of mammals. It has been labeled the "spirit molecule" due to its suspected role in the induction of dreaming, near death experiences, and vivid visionary states which may be linked to mystical or religious experiences."[27]

So there. Our pineal glands release DMT at times of spiritual visions. When DMT is released, our brains have access to the visions. Some claim this is just the brain opening itself to its own imagination of spiritual things, but my visitor pointed me to these visions arriving to us from out there, from light.

Back in 2004, when first looking around for any literature on this, the pineal gland was the commonly accepted receptor for *insight*. Historically, it is associated with seers and psychics. Today, it is a known processor of raw electromagnetic energy (that's light) and of the neurotransmitter DMT.

It seems to know when to make and release the neurotransmitter DMT, our own psychedelic spirit substance maker. On top of that spirit-door-opening function, this little gland deep inside the brain processes raw energy from light. Being so far from accessing light itself, it must get the light messages from the energy vibrations emitted by light. It is also one of the only parts of the brain not subject to the blood-brain barrier, so it does receive blood floods, and is known to release chemicals like melatonin and, now, DMT into the blood.

The pineal gland appears to be the portal and/or the catalyst through which spiritual enlightenment flows to us. DMT release is brief, intense, and with rapid onset and short duration. Therefore, DMT may not be present in the daily ongoing preparation of our brains for what is coming next, and may be reserved for the "directed visions," the insights, that come in a flash of light.

So what about the information that comes to us to guide our decisions throughout our days? When I ask the Universe to give me direction for the day, I don't have a DMT-involved psychedelic awakening. Rather, I feel beloved, and I get some direction about where to focus my energies that day. For example, "Work on the book Chapter 5" or "Clean the bathroom and we will tell you more then." Do those directions come through the pineal gland, too?

We are starting to see answers to these kinds of questions.

In 2014, the HeartMath Institute popularized the notion that the heart, not the pineal gland, is the receptor of intuition. They did a now-famous study where they found that the heart actually receives intuitive information before the brain—faster by one second or so. Pre-stimulus information from the heart is communicated to the brain.[28] But the HeartMath researchers don't rule out the role of the pineal gland when they conclude:

"On the basis of these results and those of other research, it would appear that intuitive perception is a system-wide process in which both the heart and the brain (and possibly other bodily systems) play a critical role."[29]

Other scientists, like Dr. Judith Orloff, talk about intuition starting in the whole right side of the brain, through the gut and looping into the right hippocampus, deep in the limbic system of the brain where long-term memories are thought to be stored.[30]

The work of Simon McRea pretty much supports Orloff's conclusion, at least about the brain regions involved in first intelligence through intuition. He has put together a review of many scientific studies about where intuition hits us first, and his summation points to the ventral-medial cortex region in the brain. Where's that? It's in the frontal lobe of the brain, behind the forehead. He says this is where intuitions set off neural pulses, and in particular he concludes that intuition arises in the top of the brain and moves down to the center of the brain, notably to the hippocampus, through interconnected networks.[31]

In support of the notion of intuition moving from one place to another in the brain, a Japanese researcher, Kelji Tanaka, found neural loops when he did brain scans on Shogi players (Shogi is like a chess game). These were champion players who were practiced and could rely on intuition instead of having to think about their moves. It was that same looping or interconnected networks as Simon McRea described about a top down to bottom loop in intuition. No matter where in the world intuition is studied, researchers are finding the same parts of the brain getting excited during intuition events.

Many say, after the information has looped, it arrives at the hippocampus in the emotional center of the brain. Again in Japan, two other researchers, Luo and Niki, found intuitive activity within the right hippocampus which came alive as "insight" in a task involving Japanese riddles.[32] So here again, McRea and Orloff's beliefs were substantiated. Other people point to the heart. Still others point to the Pineal Gland.

Notably, no researchers say intuitions do not arrive into the human body. In fact, some say they arrive all over the human body. Simone Wright in her book called First Intelligence proclaims "It's everywhere, it's everywhere" and she should know, not just from her studies, but also as an intuition receiver used by authorities to help in investigations. She says, "Through every organ, cell, and strand of DNA, intuition links you to the field of universal intelligence. It connects you to whatever you may desire for yourself (which is usually what the Universe desires for you, if you are listening to its guidance). She includes the skin as our largest organ to also have links to the zero point energy field where intuitions are thought to start. We have already seen in the chapter disclosing my puzzle the work of Spottiswoode and May which shows intuition as affecting skin conductance, at prestimulus moments.

Thus, intuition comes to us from the energy field and, amazingly, our energy goes back out to the field of universal intelligence in the form of our desires.[33] Although Wright says that all our biological cells operate as antenna, transmitter and receiver, with the energy field and whole body being thus used, she fancies what she calls the Trilateral Intelligence System—Brain, Gut, and Heart—to house the majority of power. Yes, the skin is a sophisticated and sensitive supercomputer, but it looks like the different systems of brain, gut, and heart, are activated in different kinds of insight.

Wright summarizes it thus: The pineal gland in the brain is particularly active during meditation and visualization practices, with a concomitant increase in "psi" (psychic events) and increased intuitive capacity generally. Meanwhile, the gut operates on a binary system, a quick yes or no. The heart communicates with the brain through nerve impulses, hormones, neurotransmitters, blood pressure waves, and through electromagnetic field interactions. If the heart wants to talk to the brain, it has quite an array of methods for doing that.[34]

Today, the definition of intuition includes not only "knowing something without conscious perception or reasoning," but also includes our body's entire psycho-physiological system in just the way Simone Wright describes it.

More researchers are finding far more generalized receptor portals than previously thought. The most notable few of these likely portals have been described above. Ultimately, it seems all our cells can be activated by intuition vibrations, "unconscious perception." This unconscious perception is evidenced not just by *FLASH!* insights, but also by subtle changes in emotions and measurable physiological changes that can be detected throughout the body, not just in the mind. There is plenty of *electrophysiological evidence of intuition*.[35]

So what do we come away with from hearing all this new scientific evidence about our reception of intuitions?

We know for certain that our subconscious minds sometimes know more than our conscious minds. Intuitions arrive all the time by an assortment of methods, perhaps even by all of them all at once, and perhaps we take the clearest message when we attend to our intuition.

For me, just knowing there is something in our bodies and our brains which could process messages from light, moved me from being a skeptic into "this is it, folks!".

Chapter 7

Above And Below, In And Out

I STARTED WITH THE PINEAL GLAND RESEARCH, and early on I concluded, if the pineal gland can receive non-sensory raw energy from light, then it is not such a leap of logic to imagine non-sensory raw energy from light being sent to it from somewhere Semanta-Laughton claimed that photons emit from black holes. Do they carry with them the light messages, since photons are little packets of light? Do they carry the messages to us, or do we go get them?

The famous physicist, Nassim Haramein, tells us we are appearing and disappearing (yes, us, we are doing this) at the speed of light and when we disappear this is how we are informed by the vacuum, and in turn we inform the vacuum; our lives and thoughts are recorded there. When we reappear, we experience the material world and the vacuum feeds us back our experience, and that is how we create our reality.[36]

Imagine the vacuum inside black holes. *There* is a possible source of the information we are sent, because black holes are known to be where matter and anti-matter alternatively pop up and down in and out of the energy field—the zero point field—with anti-matter situated in a mirror world where whatever we do might have already happened.[37] (As an aside, this would explain déjà vu, because what is happening now just happened there, and we have momentarily slipped the curtain between the two states of matter. This is purely conjecture on my part, but it makes sense with the in and outness of our energy in a mirror world.) The information from wherever it comes, moves through space faster than the speed of light.

"Space functions as an oceanic medium for subtle particles and frequencies in a similar manner to Source Intelligence. Source Intelligence is the Quantum Field that interfaces between Source and individualized consciousness. This field is the medium through which primeval Sound and Light are holographically refracted into wave-patterns."[38]

What? The Quantum Field (sometimes called the Akashic Field or the Akashic Records) is the medium within which wave patterns are formed into holograms from primeval Sound and Light? In other words, out there, in the Quantum Field, the holograms are created, reflecting what SOURCE (higher intelligence) sends.

We have seen how sound takes random particles and turns them into form (many videos on the internet show sound creating form). Sound turns matter and energy into form. So the idea of sound vibrating into the Quantum Field and creating or changing information for us, fits with all we know about how every organ in our body resonates to a certain vibration. All sound has to do is to send to us, in our signature vibrational pattern, to create and carry to us the holograms our bodies are able to (vibrationally) read.

This theory of sound is more familiar to us in Stephen Hawking's string theory where matter emanates from a multitude of strings, and each string makes different notes.[39] The harmonies I heard in my vision could have been the notes vibrating in my oscillatory wavelength, my signature vibrations. These notes presented to me harmonically were designed to tune into my portals (my skin, my heart, my brain) to receive the hologram messages coming to me. My song, as it were.

It is likely that the spinning orbs inside my vision's columns of light were the messages formed by sound, now in hologram form. In that form, I couldn't actually read them like a text message, but rather they arrived as a holographic image. Perhaps it was me interpreting the holographic images, if you will, of my home and front door and visitor and psychedelic wallpaper all in one fleeting second. With the help of the voice of my unseen visitor, I translated holograms into thoughts.

As if it isn't fantastic enough to be sent and to receive holographic messages vibrationally, it seems as if we send back energy in vibrational patterns, back into the center of Source. We emit photons from our *biophysiology* = biophotons. The power of intention causes us to emit strong enough biophotons to increase the magnetic and electric energy to effectively "send" messages holographically.[40] We emit, or send, from our hands, our stomachs, our hearts, and our brains, which are precisely the places where we receive vibrational messages.

The things we get are reciprocated by the things we send.

By now, most people know our intentions can shape our own reality, by sending to the Universe messages about what we want. These are called manifestation messages. At the same time, if we follow the messages sent to us about what the Universe wants for us, and if those two things are in harmony, with the received messages matching the sent ones, the above matching the below, we will feel in harmony with ourselves, with our world and we will manifest what we want.

Scientists, in rapid succession, confirm these findings now. It is all being newly confirmed to us, but it was not new to Thoth. Thoth was the Ancient Egyptian god of writing, magic, wisdom, and the moon. According to his worshippers (between 6000 BCE and 300 BCE), he was known as the Lord of Divine Words. He "created" a grid program of electromagnetic experience, a pyramid-shaped vehicle representing the nature of reality. His most famous quote "As above, so below" came from when he placed half of a pyramid, inverted, above the grid and said, "As is above," meaning in the nonphysical world, and half below, "As is below," in the physical world, thus creating the hourglass, or sands of time, at the center of the energy field.[41] Thoth had the knowledge that we are both above and below this electromagnetic field.

I am heartened that others are now finding Thoth was right. Nassim Haramein even says we ourselves are above then below the center of the energy field, repeatedly.

When we receive holograms we expect they are from another plane because they know more than us: another plane with information that has already happened in a mirror world? The HeartMath researchers describe "Heart Hologramming," where we should sincerely focus spirit and heart to the heart's true intent—to actualize the hologram.[42] They (the HeartMath researchers) see the incoming info as holograms like the spinning shapes I and others saw in visions.

In 2018, many are now talking about the information that comes to us as holographic. Some go so far as to say we ourselves are holograms, made of light. "Science increasingly agrees with direct human experience: we are more than the atoms and molecules of which we are composed. We are beings that emit, communicate with, and are formed from light."[43]

For the purposes of this book, it matters more that messages do come to us from light, and that we receive them in our brains' pineal glands, or in our hearts, or in our guts, or in our cells all over our bodies. The very fact that we have place(s) in our bodies where this sort of light message reception can and does occur makes my VISION credible. Even more convincing is the most recent work of William Brown, pointing to what happens to light-message-energy after it is received by the pineal gland, or the heart, or both.

Listen to the title of William Brown's 2012 work: *he Light Encoded DNA Filament and Biomolecular Quantam Communication.*[44] This research explains how inside our DNA we have tiny tubes in the center called microtubules. The job of microtubules is to transport light-energy-messages as actual light within our brains and bodies: within all our cells. Brown is taking us beyond the hologram portals of the pineal gland and/or the heart or the gut to deep inside us, to inside the deepest parts of our cells. Brown says:

> The shifting electron density of the electrical dipole produces harmonic oscillations of the pi electrons within the center of the microtubules or the DNA. Oscillating charges produce magnetic fields, and oscillating magnetic fields produce electrical fields, which produce electromagnetic waves, or in common terminology—light. This is a light encoded filament, the information-carrying strand of the DNA! Presence of these light strands is the light body of the biological organism.[45]

What this means is, because our cells are vibrating all the time, the electrical currents running through our neurons have a constantly changing positive and negative charge, creating shifts in resonance with other electrons. As the electrical energy shifts up and down, the (+,-) dipoles (energy at one end of the neuron versus the energy at the polar opposite end of the neuron) produce an oscillation. The more they shift, the greater the number and size of the oscillations. So, oscillations going from negative end, to positive end, faster and faster, create more resonance with other electrons in other neurons. The higher the energy, the more information "chatter" between neurons.

Inside our DNA, which runs throughout our brain and body, inside our cells, are tiny long tubes, "microtubules". The electrons inside the neurons plus the electrons inside these little tubes constantly shift in electrical charge density. They bond when they "match" in resonance with the oscillating electromagnetic-dipoles' activity outside the tube. The electrons form bonds, or get married to the electron who vibrates just like them. When they form what is known as a pi electron bond, they cannot rotate out of it—electrical energy outside the tube has formed a matching bond to the energy inside it. This means that when oscillations of energy coming at us from OUTSIDE the body match up with oscillations INSIDE the body, they BOND. The information in both becomes available to both, and they stay married.

The more intensely oscillating an intuition, the greater the resonance, and then the greater the message. This explains why great intuitions, great insights, come as huge light-bulbs going off in our heads, because of the magnitude of the oscillations created when those electromagnetic light messages resonate strongly with dense electrons in our DNA microtubules, which are light! Yes, those electrons are light. They are the light which bonds with, marries and carries the light messages from outside received by the pineal, gut, or heart, and they put the message inside the neural system. Therefore we feel this thunderclap all through our bodies via the light-encoded DNA. At least, that's my conclusion, based on Brown's work, explaining how, when we are suddenly enlightened, it thrills us through and through. Flash!

But, you might wonder, have I taken this too far? Does Brown think the light in his light-encoded DNA microtubules contains messages? Well, Brown thinks all our information, not just insight and intuition, is carried about in our brains by these microtubules (as if light messages are sent to us for everything we think and do).

He says: "The brain only acts as an interface for the purely energetic aspects of sentience transduced into the physical experience."[46]

More simply, brains receive electromagnetic light energy as consciousness, making it available to our physical bodies. He goes on to explain:

"This means that the brain has never produced a thought, and never will, because that is not what the brain does...

it is simply a categorization of the Information field, which is a part of the Unified Field. So it is a non-physical component of the mind that accesses the non-physical Information field—this can be referred to as the higher mind... and it accesses this Information field... allowing the physical mind to perceive the electromagnetic lightwave patterns, the holograms, as thoughts."[47]

Brown is asserting that not just the intuitions of ideas/insights/benevolent guidance come to us from the Zero Point Field, but all our thoughts do the same.

There is the idea that goes so far as to say we are but energy, light-energy packets, manifested as holograms, visible only through light being shined upon us.[48] Some have recently been popularizing this idea of a holographic universe in which we are but thoughts (light energy): For example:

Thought materializes (reality) on this planet as vibrating light (or holograms) brought in through an electrical frequency (vibration/sound).[49]

Thus, light waves bring us our thoughts, beginning with sound vibrations which form the holograms which come to us through light.

Just as interesting as William Brown seeing light waves in DNA, others are discovering they can **hear** sounds inside DNA. Dr. Peter Gariaev is the founder of Wave Genetics. Wave Genetics uses resonant sound waves, beamed at the DNA, to change genetic traits and even heal damaged genes.[50]

About harmonic sounds in our DNA, Gariaev says:

"In aqueous solution, DNA molecules produce a continuous sound. They create a complex melody with recurrent musical phrases."[51]

Brown took us inside DNA molecules and showed us Light, and now Gariaev takes us to the same place and shows us Sound. For Gariaev, there are messages in the sounds. Therefore, we have both light and sound waves vibrating within us in our DNA strands. Coincidentally, in my VISION, I saw that we have both light and sound waves coming towards us. These waves are outside our bodies everywhere, and now we know they are also inside our bodies. As above, so below.

We are energetically connected to the intelligence field which is all around us, around all of us at the same time, and we are energetically connected to everyone else in the Universe similarly surrounded by the vibrational energy of the intelligence field. Sound vibrations create the connections to be sent. Light transports the messages.

> "Eastern philosophers and metaphysicists have understood for millennia; the inner nature of everything is Sound. How does sub-quantum light and sound coalesce to create FORM, as nervous system signals, as dreams, visions, and inspiration?"

That question was posed and answered by Bluntaday. [52]

"Sound waves have been proven to generate geometric forms in matter. Waveforms can be sculpted to enter biogenetic fields, restore cellular health and trigger encoded electromagnetic fields within cells of the Central Nervous System (CNS)."

That is how Gariaev uses sound therapy to heal diseases.[53] He sculpts waveforms to enter biogenetic fields.

Gariaev is not the only one using sound to heal. Sound is also used to invite energy into the chakras.[54] The chakras are energy centres within us. There is an "Interface Zone" between the human instrument and the vibratory soup which supports the human instrument's mission and purpose... to achieve coherence in the vibrations."[55] That coherence is what my visiting stranger called "harmony."

Light and Sound vibrations interface between First Source (the Universe) and human reception of holographic ideas (intuitions). Getting in harmony with those vibrations is our mission. In other words, finding coherence.

Coherence includes sending "back" light messages.

"... the human body emits ultraweak photon emissions (UPEs), with a visibility 1,000 times lower than the sensitivity of our naked eye. While not visible to us, these particles of light (or waves, depending on how you are measuring them) are part of the visible electromagnetic spectrum and are detectable via sophisticated modern instrumentation."[56]

Thus, DNA is light-encoded and full of harmonious sound, coming to and going out from us. The brilliant lights and the beautiful rhapsody of the Universe are within us. Just think of how we speak of someone who has high energy when we say they are bright sparks, beams of sunlight... we see their bright light as they emanate exciting, high oscillating emotions, thoughts, a beaming presence.

Our thoughts are at least as much created in the energy field as they are within our minds. In fact, perhaps none of them are created by us alone. In turn, it is suspected that all our thoughts, ideas, etc. are beamed back to the Zero Point Field, long known as the place where all our thoughts and deeds are recorded and kept, as energy.

Interestingly, no one can find memory inside the brain. They can find six places where memory is processed, but not where memories are stored. The hippocampus, which we saw earlier as a portal for arriving holograms, is still thought by some to be the place where long-term memories are stored, but we know memory isn't kept there because damage to this brain area does not eliminate long-term memories. Rather, it is now thought that memories are stored in the Akashic Field, and light is the conductor for the receiving and sending of the memory retrievals.

The work of Dr. Jacobo Grinberg Zylberbaum speaks of the energy field as having columns and rows, with information sitting on the interstices, and that is how we construct our memories, from accessing those crossings of information—we send out a query for the thought or memory, and at the crossroads of energy where that memory is stored, the query and the information hook up and it is sent back to us:

> "The interaction between the neural field and space creates a pattern of interference that is called the energetic structure of experience…interaction occurs between the energy structure of experience and a central process…"[57]

I like to think the columns of colored light I saw set boundaries around the individualized energy fields, so that the holograms didn't collide or spill over into each other, so that each sent memory or thought was clear and not contaminated by bits of other nearby memories. These boundaries between the light columns could be set up at the interstices of the energy field from whence the messages are sent. Thus, one holographic message inside one light column could have arisen from one energy crosspoint, and another in a different light column from another crosspoint, each activated by Sound and moved by light. Grinberg described the interstices as "consciousness"—the points of information and memory, the place where receiving and sending match up and energize the required information to be sent to us.

Grinberg's idea that memory and consciousness exist in some energy field outside of our bodies was contentious. His work was becoming famous when, in December of 1994, he was last seen being trundled into the hatchback of a small car in Mexico City, where he worked as a Psychology Professor at the Autonomous University of Mexico City, and he has never been seen again.

The results of Grinberg's studies validate the phrase, *"As above, so below."* We get from above, and match it with, bind it with, what is below, and we send back (from "below") our conscious energy to "above," to the grid. These informations meet at the interstices.

Once inside us, however, we have the question "Where does this light and music travel to when it goes along those microtubules, taking elctromagnetic waves somewhere inside us?" Remember:

> "Electromagnetic waves are nothing else but light!"—Trinh Xuan Thuan (Chaos and Harmony. Oxford University Press. 2001)

Electromagnetic waves, or light, bring messages to us, so that our brains know in advance what is coming any second now. But how does the brain deal with that advance knowledge?

After a long search, I finally found physical evidence of brains knowing in advance what is coming. I found out about the amazing concept: *preafference*.

With preafference, it really doesn't matter where it arrives first: the heart, the pineal gland, or all over us, or whether it comes from above or below. Without *preafference*, the messages would go nowhere in our brains. Just think about *preafference* and the elegance of the brain as you now learn about it.

Chapter 8

There it is! PREAFFERENCE

AT FIRST I FOUND NO LITERATURE tackling the issue of the brain knowing stuff in advance. Eventually, an older text called Information in the Brain, by Dr. Ira B. Black (from 1994), had a section that talked about neuronal receptors in places NOT along the neuronal train pathway, but situated before the train would need to be electrically moved along. He wrote:

"Receptors are not restricted to the postsynaptic membrane but are also present in the presynaptic membrane."[58]

How odd! Before we shunt off our neuronal train on its electrical journey to the next thought, before that train moves along, there is something that is called an "autoreceptor" found just before the place from whence the train will get supercharged further along its journey. Dr. Black is saying before the synapse occurs, there are some receptors which he calls autoreceptors. Before the synapse! Before the place where information jumps from one cell to the next, are some other receptors not belonging to the train. Something in the now-visited cell's membrane receives some sort of information prior to that cell receiving the other entrained information it is supposed to receive. These newly discovered autoreceptors *have* to be receiving *some sort* of information, or else why are there? Well Black thinks because they "talk to" the other receptors, communicate with them, direct them. Black reported activity on the presynaptic membrane *changes* whether or not the neuron releases neurochemicals to synapse at all. Autoreceptors appear to be the local boss of the synapse, telling it to open for this imminent info, or stay shut. That pre-information decides whether or not you are going to run that particular neuronal train at all.

> "Activation of these receptors alters the subsequent release of transmitters by the presynaptic neuron..."[59]

To reiterate: Black was saying, when these before-synapse receptors are activated, they change the subsequent chemical release from that neuron. These presynaptic receptors alter the "receptivity" to the information that is coming along right now. And these receptors activate before the synapsing neuron is aroused, before it is called to action.

This means the presynaptic receptors tell whether the cell should or should not, receive the info that is headed its way. Before the neural train pulls into the station, the stationmaster receptors on the presynaptic membrane decide which spur lines to open and which to close. Therefore, there is a stationmaster! With a plan. So, there is a plan for all this. It's not just random thoughts and information speeding from cell to cell. Cells get a tiny moment to decide to decide to get involved or not, in each particular train ride.

> "...the neuron communicates with itself through stimulation of these 'autoreceptors'."[60]

The stationmaster directs the plan. The neuronal train follows that plan only after having a little talk with itself about whether this is the plan for *it*. The neuronal train itself does not make that decision, the plan does. The plan was hatched and being conducted before we even thought about it at all. That is the role of autoreceptors, to relay the plan.

But Dr. Black and other scientists didn't talk about what an autoreceptor might be all about within an information processing paradigm. Nor why would we have them. Much of the above is inferential regarding neural entrainments, given presynaptic autoreceptors. I kept looking for someone who must know about the process.

Three years after THE VISION, I came across what is now the most dog-eared little book that I own, called *How Brains Make Up Their Minds,* by Dr. Walter J. Freeman, published in 1999. It is now a dated book, but I haven't found one that tackles this issue as fully as he does. He introduces the term, Preafference:

"The mind constructs **goal states** which guide the body through complex sequences of actions. The senses are primed to select the smells, sights, sounds and tastes that are predicted by impending goal directed actions."

Freeman calls this goal-state-construction **preafference**, which we experience as **attention and expectation**.

"**Preafference** allows our minds to predict specifically how the action to be taken will change the relations of knowing (through the eyes, ears, nose, tastebuds, and fingers). The messages it sends out to our senses are called corollary discharges. (So, these corollary discharges are what Dr.Black saw on the presynaptic membrane.) Preafference is the process by which we imagine what things may be like, if or when they come.[61]

Suddenly, there it was—preafference: the process by which our imagination, our intuition, our insights, set up the goal states in our brains. It is the process by which light-encoded messages can move along our DNA and into our neurons to pre-alert and pre-assemble the pathways, those specific neuronal train routes (out of the billions the brain could choose), to achieve the goals of our imagining.

Through light messages and the process of preafference acting on auto-receptors, we already have in mind what we will think about, and what we plan to do about it, before we actually think about it.

Recently, using brain scans as they watch subjects make decisions, neuroscientists conclude that our neurons fire up to plan and organize a goal-directed action (that is, set in motion preafference autoreceptors) anywhere between about a *quarter of a second before,* and right up to seven full seconds before we are even aware of our intention.[62] Interestingly, at the same time the heart rate deceleration prior to future emotional stimuli is at that time communicated to the brain."[63]

Findings like these back up Freeman's (1999) theory that the organism has some idea of what it is "looking" for, and this idea is formed in the imagination, and it precedes search and perception.

Freeman's notion of pre-awareness neural firing—*preafference*—is central to understanding how the brain works at all in response to how messages which come to us in light might be hosted, organized and enacted within us. Preafference processes are the evidence required to prove the pre-existence of thoughts in our brains before we realize we are thinking those thoughts.

Preafference proves my stranger was right! Messages come to us from somewhere... Flash! From light. Preafference now kicks in and our brains prepare to act on those messages.

Furthermore, re-looking now at the recent findings of how we emit biphotons, researchers show that "...light stimulation can generate biophotons that move along the neural fibers, *probably as neural communication signals.*"[64] So, this is how preafference works—messages encoded in light, carried through the microtubules in our DNA, arrive at our brains which preselect from the billions of neurons (via preafference), the thought trains relevant to the messages we are receiving. Preafference creates the entrainment routings to prepare for the message's journey to its enactment.

To recap: our heart, our brain, our skin, maybe all of those at once, receive non-sensory electromagnetic light messages which activate the light-encoding in our DNA, which is the routing required for preafference to fire up the correct pathways, readying them to prime a message to go from one neuronal station to another, and then to an act (an action, a thought, a conversation), all in a heartbeat, faster than the speed of light. It's an elegant system to interface communication between us and an energy field with greater information than we own

Many mystics have pointed to improved insight from received knowledge that does not come to us from our senses. Extrasensory knowledge seems to hold importance in developing peace and centeredness. To align, or become coherent with, or get in harmony with, knowledge which is given to us as intuition is beneficial for us.

Everything within our bodies has a beneficial role for our health and survival. If we have the equipment to receive messages from light, then it makes sense that we would benefit from getting in sync with those messages. Whatever our built-in equipment that we use in receiving electromagnetic oscillations' information, we should benefit from it—it is all purposeful.

The stranger communicated to me that when we get messages from light, and obey them, our lives go well. Thus, when we are aware of the messages in the light, and listen to them, we are respecting our body. A healthy body includes a healthy respect for insights and intuitions. Sound and light messages are busy all the time, and the happiest people among us demonstrate trust in the habit of getting in harmony with intuitions, to achieve coherence with the Universe's intentions for us. Harmony.

Chapter 9

An Inborn Will To Harmony

MESSAGES RECEIVED VIA INTUITION, or instinct/insight, are usually more compelling, more "sure" than thoughts engendered by logic. All the time, people say, "I don't know what came over me, I just had to do it and the result was wonderful!" It is as if the drive to obey insights is greater than the urge ignore them (it is a not a level playing field—insights weigh in more urgently than other thoughts). We actually have to make a decision to ignore them, to not pay attention to them, when we let reasoning override them. Really, it is as if we have an inborn will to harmonize with them: a coherence drive.

Harmony drives are seen everywhere in nature. Fireflies in a mob can suddenly begin flashing on and off at the same time. There is a widely circulating video online of 32 metronomes (pendulums) spontaneously synchronizing. We all prefer social gatherings where everyone is in harmony, as opposed to being at odds with each other. Even within us, more than just in our brains, we have harmony: the heart's natural pacemaker is a cluster of about 10,000 cells whose job is to generate the rhythm that commands the rest of the heart to beat. If it stops working in sync, it experiences arrythmia and the heart goes into crisis. When it does work, no one cell acts as the lead rhythm setter. They all work in harmony.

Fireflies, the heart—these are but two examples of what scientists describe as one of the most pervasive drives in the universe, the tendency to synchronize, to resonate in harmony. Neurons in the brain act similarly. A flash of insight can be seen on a brain scan as literally a burst of electrical synchrony, an instant where the separate parts of the brain begin to harmonize.

I am not the first person to notice and think about an inborn Will to Harmony, although I have not heard it called that. Others call it coherence, while still others, like Deepak Chopra, talk of the Law of Least Effort:

> "Nature's intelligence functions with effortless ease ... with carefreeness, harmony, and love. And when we harness the forces of harmony, joy, and love, we create success and good fortune with effortless ease."[65]

This law has sometimes been mistaken as permission to be lazy, to not strive for excellence, to make no effort at all in life. But that is not what it is. Rather, it is to *not fight* instinct, to not suppress good ideas just because you don't know where they came from. It is to not go against harmony, which would cause us to suffer in our brains something like what the heart suffers as arrythmia when it gets out of harmony: chaos, confusion, "not knowing" if something is the right thing to do, second guessing. The Law of Least Effort is to make no effort to go against insights.

Instead of the term Least Effort, I prefer to speak of an innate Will to Harmony—which is the unmistakable and hard-to-counteract drive to synchronize with what is naturally coming down the pipe for us, for our benevolent development.

Further, to better access intuition and get in harmony with it, there are ways to quiet the brain activity, and one of most popular of these is meditation. Meditation gives cleaner access to energy messages by calming fears, by quelling neural chaos.

"The more we meditate, the less anxiety we have, and it turns out this is because we're actually loosening the connections of particular neural pathways."[66] Stephen Strogatz, who wrote Sync: The Emerging Science of Spontaneous Order, would say we automatically will be loosening those connections so we can create order in the brain.[67]

As Strogatz's reviewer, John Wiswell says, "Strogatz's fundamental point is that many things in our world exhibit spontaneous and often shocking synchrony. Those thousands of fireflies flashing in perfect unison in California, the human brain synchronizing sleep cycles to body temperature cycles, bridges swaying and distributing force primarily in one direction despite all the trampling feet moving it in sundry directions—we are surrounded by seemingly self-organizing systems of order."[68]

Achieving coherence with messages that come to us in light is an example of how to create order for ourselves out of chaos. Out of the billions of distracting thoughts, ideas, and images, intuition guides us to pay attention to the one thing that will help at this moment. Whatever we can do to help ourselves come to harmonic order is beneficial.

Those who meditate a lot have increased awareness of light messages, increased in-tuneness with inner thoughts, increased order instead of chaos. They have constant access to their intuition if they want it.

There seem to be at least two kinds of intuition: the "Flash! problem-solved (now-tell-about-it) sudden insight" kind, and there is the kind of intuition that is not a flash, but intuition based on willful access to a sure state of knowing without reasoning. This kind may be a load of smaller flashes, but to attend to this intuition, meditation helps.

Those who are unable to meditate can still get into a brainwave state that supports attention to intuition. As you will see in Chapter 12, it is possible to use an EEG machine to fast track into meditation for those who have difficulty meditating. In whatever way you access your messages, follow them. Resist overriding them. They are there for your good health, well-being, and soul development. They will help you create order from the vast array of stimuli that bombards you. They will bring you inner harmony.

PART IV

Accessing and Using Intuition

SINCE MY UNSEEN VISITOR'S appearance in my life, many experts in the field of Intuition have published information about HOW to increase access of it, and WHY that is beneficial. Some of their books appear in Appendix A. Most of these encourage us to seek the coherence of harmony, the inner peace that comes with accessing our intuition. There is, however, at least one further extremely useful function of intuition beyond saving our own individual butts from danger, or creating coherence within us. The next section is devoted to using intuition to promote health and tranquility in others, in particular through Remote Viewing.

Remote Viewing is a term coined by Russell Targ, an American physicist, parapsychologist and author who became known for early developmental work in lasers and laser applications. He joined the Stanford Research Institute (the SRI) in 1972 where he worked for the CIA and Army Intelligence in locating places and things. He distinguished between clairvoyance, seeing into the future, and this thing he called "Remote Viewing" which is the practice of seeking impressions about a distant or unseen target using parapsychological means. He suggests that remote viewing is not a rare psychic ability, but can be trained in people who have interest, simply by quieting their minds and looking: anything you see in that state he calls "nonlocal perception."[69]

As far as I know, Targ does not use remote viewing to heal people. However, many remote viewers can and do just that: heal people. This next chapter is contributed by someone who practices "Remote Viewing and Remote Healing." People contact her to discover what it is about their health she can see that Doctors can't.

Chapter 10

Remote Viewing and Healing

(Chapter Contributed by Nicole Meyers Henderson, Remote Viewer, NC, USA)

We know this, with repeat practice the intuitive genius within the brain gets exercised, becoming more sophisticated and precise. Just think, as we choose a specific field of study and fully immerse ourselves in it, the Caudate Nucleus gets exercised, "strengthening a muscle." so to speak, and our intuitive genius takes over. The muscle doesn't have to "think" as it performs while the neuronal train moves along automatically. Contemplate the amount of time it takes for a med student to become a doctor. Once licensed, after 10 or more years of training a physician will have graduated to a state whereby they are able to look at their patient and intuitively pinpoint what's wrong with them, sometimes only after a cursory scan. Or, a skilled art teacher at an estate sale who finds an old painting under a pile of rubbish, sees the signature of a famous artist inscribed on the lower right hand corner, but intuitively knows the painting is a fake just by looking at the brushstrokes.

When the brain is exercised properly, we learn to trust what we sense, which allows us to make spontaneous decisions at the blink of an eye without needing to perform a more thorough analysis. Thus, as well as "flashes of light going off in our heads," intuition can be defined as "influence" from the body or brain emerging first as instinctive feelings or sensations. There is experimental support for this definition of intuition.

On May 20, 2016, author Cari Nierenberg, a Live Science contributor, declared that researchers have found evidence that people using intuition "make faster, more accurate and confident decisions";[70] findings of which have been published online in the Journal of Psychological Science. Joel Pearson, associate professor of Psychology at University of New South Wales Australia, suggests this same study[71] shows that intuition does in fact exist and researchers are now better able to measure it. All living creatures possess what seems to be a supernatural ability to intuitively sense things.

I am sure you have all heard twin stories like the twin living in North Carolina who feels a sharp pain in her right pointer finger as her sister, who lives in Michigan, cuts the exact finger down to the bone with a knife. There are so many stories of intuition and supernatural abilities to sense things.

I have spent years in deep contemplation about this; asking questions such as, what is responsible for our intuitive urgings? Is it something inside of us that provokes these experiences, or is it something outside of us, within our environment? Is it really a psychic experience that cannot be explained or can our sensory body and our brain be the cause of such experiences?

I think sometimes it's more exciting to believe that these events are mystical rather than accidental coincidences. Many people experience intuitive 'hits' and seem perfectly happy not knowing how they do it or where those hits come from. How often do you hear people talk about knowing what their spouse was about to say before they say it? Or how often have you had an experience with knowing who is on the other end of the phone when it rings? We all, at one point in our lives, have experienced intuition in one way or another.

Advancements within the fields of Neuroscience, Quantum Theory, Physics, Energy Transference and Cell Communication research now help us better understand the complexities and connections associated with our sensory system and our environments. This book has been quite thorough in sharing the science behind intuition. My contribution to this work is proof that we sentient beings can use our sensory abilities in ways that can surpass intuition: ways which are often not talked about in scientific circles. *I use remote viewing exercises in concert with my sensory abilities daily for myself as well as my clients.*

I am excited to reaffirm what has been shared so far in this book about the works of Einstein, as well as the successfully documented theories that other scientists disclosed, which pre-date the 1800s and on which scientists still rely today. Amalgamating old theories with new puzzle pieces shared by modern day physicists and cosmologists may help us transcend old paradigms of thought; thoughts that are self-limiting, unfavorably influencing our behavior, causing us to believe that we must rely upon outside authorities and agencies to make decisions that can have long-standing negative effects on our lives and on the lives of those we care for. Utilizing tools such as Remote Viewing can teach us how to truly trust that innate wisdom which resides within the cells of our body as well as within all atoms, molecules, particles and energy fields which surround us.

Energy is the universal language. When we are able to decipher or decode the streams of information coming to us in the form of energy, there is nothing for us to wonder about: merely hold the intention to extract pure information from the Source and the truth is streamed *in its purest form.*

I will conclude this opening by sharing my belief about intuition. It is not something to fear, but instead should be embraced and nurtured. Intuition is a brain process that cooperates with the cellular structure of the body to measure inside and outside stimuli, giving us the ability to make decisions without the use of analytical reasoning. The big news is: **anyone can do it!**

Remote Viewing History

We all have our own set of perceptive skills which enable us to accurately experience (sense, feel, see, taste, smell, hear) and describe detailed and accurate information on any event, person, being, place, or object that has ever existed, or does exist, or will exist. For those who do not believe they can tap into their intuitive self, Remote Viewing protocols can take you where most have never gone. There are no limits to its uses. Its practices allow the viewer to live in full awareness, which opens the user up to accurately experience and describe events, people and objects (present, past and future). It's a conditioning discipline that teaches you to stay totally with your subtle senses in a pure and innocent way, without "jumping in" too quickly with your intellect and imagination. It is a deepening tool that integrates the spirit, mind, and body, especially when combined with other disciplines that are used for growth (e.g. meditation, prayer, yoga, martial arts, etc.). Remote viewing may totally and positively expand your view of consciousness and alter your known reality.

The Stanford Research Institute developed remote viewing for the Army and Defense Intelligence Agency. It was used in a secret espionage program for 20 years. Many Army personnel received training in Remote Viewing. Protocols have now been refined to allow trained remote viewers to be consistent, detailed and accurate in their descriptions of target people, places and things. It could be considered a distant cousin to some other psychic disciplines, with the main difference being the extremely high and consistent accuracy and inter-rater reliability.

"Teams" of remote viewers can approach 100% accuracy as they can become "bilocated," where a viewer makes a strong "target" contact with all of their senses. This allows the viewer to feel as if they are inside of, or in the vicinity of, the target. It is quite exhilarating to perform remote viewing that so accurately concurs with the physical evidence later matched to the viewing. You do not go into a trance, nor will you astral travel, nor will you "channel" an outside force. It is simply a way to tap into your natural intuitive abilities and move beyond them to become one with that which you are remotely viewing.

What it is

Remote Viewing is a tool which allows us to move beyond space and time, to sift through layers of extraneous noise, to tap into other realms of consciousness for gathering essential information that will aid others in restoring balance to their lives, or rebalance our own. Methods of viewing allow us to tap into any realm of consciousness, subject matter, space, or time, for the purpose of extracting information for our own personal growth, health, and well-being, or for that of others. Remote viewing is about data retrieval. We enter the Universal Energy highway with a pure intention to extract truthful information and the Universe responds by unlocking its secret cache.

It is debatable about who the real founders of Remote Viewing are, however there is a known record of Harold Puthoff and Russell Targ creating their program in the spring of 1972. It is only fair to say at this point, although I have not included their works, remote viewing has been used by Native American Indians for thousands of years, but was not referenced as such. Also noted, but not elaborated upon, is research done in 1979 within the Princeton Engineering Anomalies Research (PEAR) at Princeton University, by Robert G. Jahn and Brenda Dunne, who pursued rigorous scientific studies of the interaction of human consciousness with sensitive physical devices, systems and processes, testing psychokinesis and remote perception. Remote Viewing's success and history is now, 50 years later, well established. Let's call it RV from now on.

It is inherent within humans to wish to understand our world and beyond, to long for growth and expansion. In order to do that, we must detach from those things that detract from out attention, the things that distract us—the noise, static, and life stresses. Centering, or focusing oneself on a particular target subject without letting our ego take part can be a huge undertaking. RV's practical applications allow this centering to occur. Its techniques and protocols were created to cut through the noise, allowing us to tap into non-conventional environments at will, to extract information—permitting the viewer to intimately and genuinely know someone, to walk a thousand miles in their shoes, to feel what they feel, to see what they see, to understand what is going on in their present life and even determine why they have chosen a particular life path. Viewers can get so close to someone that they can energetically become one with the target of focus, fully grasping the target's involvement in the world.

RV is an instrument, a tool that allows us to take a leap into oneness with all that exists, for the purposes of acquiring or expanding our consciousness; merging with the quantum consciousness, for communication, healing, growth, and enlightenment.

More than 100 years ago scientists began their quest to legitimize claims relating to the presence of sensory perception: perceptual abilities whereby individuals were able to recognize and explain data that was retrieved without going to a specific location, or without being in the same room with a person or thing that needed to be examined. This scientific inquiry began within the field of parapsychology in the United States as well as abroad. Its nature was examined within the Electronic and Bioengineering Laboratory of Stanford Research Institute, investigating the abilities of inexperienced and experienced volunteers to "view"[72] remote technical targets which included buildings, roads, laboratory apparatuses, and geography for determining the quality and accuracy of perception. In 1995 the CIA released declassified documents disclosing its sponsorship of the 1970s program of RV which had been performed, to determine whether the phenomena of RV would "have any utility for intelligence collection."

Programs such as the *Stargate Project*[73] were kept classified until April of 1995 when an executive order was issued by President Clinton, entitled "Classified National Security Information." The document's main focus was to create openness in an effort to emphasize their commitment to a more open Government. Starting in 1995, Puthoff, the founder and acting Director (1972-85), discussed the genesis of the program and reported on some of the early, declassified results. The program was a "multi-year, multi-site, multi-million dollar effort. Originally, though, Puthoff had simply circulated a proposal in an effort to gain funding for research related to quantum biology, to determine whether physical theory was capable of describing life processes. He was just suggesting doing measurements involving plants and lower organisms.[74] His widely circulated proposal met with the eyes of Cleve Backster in New York City, who already measured the electrical activity of plants with standard polygraph equipment. While visiting Backster's lab, an artist by the name of Ingo Swann just happened to see Puthoff's proposal. Writing to Puthoff, Swann noted his interest in investigating the boundary between the physics of the animate and inanimate, and inquired about giving consideration to experiments of a parapsychological nature.

During his visit to the laboratory, Swann seemed to disturb the operating magnetometer which was located in a vault below the floor of the building, shielded by an aluminum container with copper shielding as well as a superconducting shield. Swann then went on to remote view the interior of the equipment and drew a reasonable facsimile of its construction. Puthoff documented Ingo Swann's feat.

Due to increasing concern within the intelligence community about a Soviet-funded parapsychological program, the government was "on the lookout for a research laboratory outside of academia that could handle a quiet, low-profile classified investigation"[75] in which they would administer simple experiments with Swann. The tests revolved around Swann attempting to describe the contents of a box that visitors had hidden objects in.

> In one test Swann said "I see something small, brown, and irregular, sort of like a leaf or something that resembles it, except that it seems very much alive, like it's even moving!" The target chosen by one of the visitors turned out to be a small live moth... looking much like a leaf.[76]

The results were impressive enough that an eight month $49,909 Biofield Measurement Program was negotiated linking laser colleague Russell Targ to the program. Thus was the beginning of official RV.

Then soon followed corroborating work by those researchers, Jahn and Dunne of PEARS at Princeton University who, in addition to studying remote perception, now studied psychokinesis effects on electronic random generators, successfully linking subjects' intentions and random results.[77] RV was further studied by Jahn in 1982 where he published a thorough review of psychic occurrences from an engineering perspective.[78]

It has long been a matter of philosophical investigation as to whether a human's ability to perceive distinctive features of space is totally an acquired ability or is exclusively innate, attributable to genetic factors, by way of some sensory apparatus. As described in my own prior works, *Cellular Memory and Cellular Memory Detoxification*,[79] I was able to determine that our perceptual (or better still, our sensory) systems are fed information continuously because we are sentient—perhaps hardwired as vast sensation-driven apparatuses, much like that of a super computer which sends and receives data 24 hours each day. Because we are bombarded with an overabundance of stimuli during a day's time, the question we must ask is not "What data can we obtain from our environment or things?" but rather, "How do we handle the stimulus or data the body receives?"

The answer lies not within our limited capabilities but on "what" we choose to focus our attention. Any information can be processed effectively, impartially, and without prejudices, but in limited amounts. Therefore, it becomes essential for an individual to selectively focus on "relevant stimuli and reject distracting and extraneous ones."[80] One has to be intentionally selective to remote view. The best way is to attend to intuitions. Let intuition serve as the cogent agent of where our attention should focus.

To briefly circle back to intuition I will share some of my personal experiences which allowed me to develop my abilities.

In my youth, I learned hard lessons that taught me to trust what I was sensing. At age 10, I spent the summer on my best friend's farm playing and helping with their farm animals. On one warm summer morning I hung on the barnyard fence watching my bestie and her brother-in-law bottle feed a newborn calf that was unable to nurse from its mother. As I turned my attention away from the soft cuddly nursing calf and on to its mother; a husky bovine bundle of dirt and stink, a dark yet thick meandering pain traveled through the frontal lobe of my brain causing a sick feeling in my stomach. The cow was angry and my body knew it. Sensing something was about to happen, I yelled out to my friend to tell her to get out of the barnyard. She turned to look at me, smiled and shrugged as if dismissing my concern just as the mother cow leapt on top of her, striking the back of her neck and head, bucking forward and back like an angry bull trying to get a cowboy off of its back. My friend's eyes were as big as saucers as she tried to escape the cow's pounding hooves. The pain in my head and the sick feelings that registered within my body tipped me off to what was about to happen but there was nothing I could do to stop it. Fortunately her brother-in-law jumped in to snatch her out from under the cow just before she struck again.

In my mid 20's, I began working with families and police in finding missing children. I located several over the span of a few years. I could never have imagined that I would be able to do such things. I could feel what each victim had gone through in life, as well as what they endured during their death experience. I spent countless hours obsessing over the lives lost, never really feeling as if I had made an ounce of difference. Their experiences flowed through the cells of my body making it difficult to focus or think about living my own life. I spent three years lost in sadness and pain, pondering my own mortality because of the deaths of those I was trying to help. Fearing I would lose myself, I chose to step away from this particular work, although I quickly learned that there was no way to truly escape. I had to learn how to use the abilities in a totally different way and not try to block out or protect myself from the things I disliked or feared. I never intended to do such work, and it was a far cry from my earlier first major realization that I could RV, which came about when I was suddenly able to see inside the workings of a car!

In 1994, my father introduced me to the NASCAR industry, where he and his team spent hundreds of thousands of dollars, and hour upon hour, getting their cars ready for weekly races. One day, while hanging out with the team in their garage stall, the hum and vibration of the racecar engines lulled me into a meditative-like state. I closed my eyes and leaned on the racecar to take the load off of my aching feet. I could hear the guys talking, mulling over scenarios in order to give the driver what he needed out of the car. I remember thinking about not knowing much about racecars, but while thinking about the motor and any potential engine issues, a virtual map of the inner workings of the car appeared in my mind's eye. Entirely by accident, a new world opened to me, creating a huge chasm between what I thought I knew to be true about life and a new unsettling perspective that would fracture any semblance of normal I had experienced previously. How did I stumble into this virtual world? What did I do that I had not done before?

By leaning against the car and focusing on helping the team make the race, the car somehow answered my thoughts. What appeared in my mind's eye was a picture of the engine linked to a mishmash of electrical wires that ran from the motor down the center of the car within the driver compartment. My heartbeat quickened as I heard electric-like sparks which then suddenly faded just as I felt the engine lose power. Since this was my first experience with seeing, hearing and feeling a race car, I did not trust the information, so instead of sharing what I saw and heard I chose to keep the experience to myself. As the team worked harder and faster to get ready, I forgot that it had happened. That afternoon the team ran their qualifying round and managed to place at the back of Sunday's racing field.

Sunday came quickly. It was a sunny but cool morning at Darlington Motor Speedway in South Carolina when the driver took command of the Active Motorsports #32 Winston Cup race car. Team members suited up and headed onto the track for driver introductions. As my father moved off toward the race hauler to watch the race, he handed a headset to me and motioned for me to put it on so that I could hear the team and driver interactions. Placing them over my ears, I wandered off to find an out-of-the-way spot to watch the race. Mid way through the race I felt a spike in my energy along with a quickening of my heartbeat. Without provocation I began to hear the same spark-like sound that I had when I was leaning against the race car in the garage area the day before. I started to feel anxious, wondering where the sound was coming from. At one point, I got so freaked out by the energy I was feeling I couldn't swallow the saliva in my mouth. As I heard the noise repeat, I felt the motor lose power. My heart began to race so fast I thought I was going to pass out. Then something within me started putting the pieces together. I realized that the sound had to do with engine power and the energy dying off was the race car losing power. I was so scared I began to walk away from the racetrack and then, as if responding to my anxiety and inner query, the driver's excited voice sounded over the headset.

"I've lost power and I don't know why."

"Try to get her started again," said the crew chief.

The voices fell silent for a second, then the driver keyed the mic. "Nothing, she won't start," as a few race cars passed him on the track like he was standing still.

At that exact moment, a vision of the car map showed up in my mind's eye again, just like it had done on Saturday before their qualifying run. This time, it showed me the same tangle of wires that ran down the center of the car but this time it revealed that they ran into a box positioned to the right of the driver. I could see that a wire had come loose from the power box. For a millisecond, I thought about keying up the mic to tell the driver where to look. Then apprehension set in.

Fearing how the team would react, I hesitated, then I realized that by speaking up I might help them finish the race. I moved to click in to tell the driver to check for a disconnected wire to the power box and just as I touched the button the driver keyed in and spoke.

"The wire to the power box is disconnected. I got it!" He quickly reconnected the wire and fired the engine just in time to finish the race.

So how did this happen?

I leaned on the car and it showed up in my mind like an X-ray or MRI image. Interestingly, this was not my first experience with a technique known as psychometry although it was my first truly life enhancing and transformative encounter.

Psychometry

Psychometry is how it happened. This technique, also known as psychoscopy, is considered to be a form of extrasensory perception characterized by the ability to make sensible, or logical, associations by making physical contact with an animated or inanimate object. In other words, by touching some-thing (an object) or some-other being (a person, or an animal), we can make associations not otherwise available to us.

The word was coined by Joseph Rodes Buchanan in 1842, when he came up with the notion that all things give off an emanation. "The past is entombed in the present," said Buchanan in 1843, believing that all things of this world are an enduring monument. In 1885, he published the *Manual of Psychometry: the Dawn of a New Civilization*, in which he detailed how direct knowledge of psychometry would be applied to, and affect various branches of science, elevate schools of philosophy and art, and further influence wide social change by enlightening humanity.

Although there have been, and still are, cynics who believe psychometry to be a pseudo-science, I draw from a wellspring of information; my own innate understanding that resides within the cells of my body (my personal experiences) and scientific sleuths of physics, cosmology and molecular biology.

Over the many adolescent and adult years of my life, I questioned the universe and how it works. I remember never feeling quite settled with the word psychic and I also remember how people responded to me when I shared my premonitions and spiritual insights. My questioning mind prevailed, and the Universe responded by awakening me to others who were also moved by unseen forces, the most notable being Albert Einstein, who was moved by unseen forces to attempt to construct a theory explaining all the laws of nature, from atom to galaxy. Many have been inspired by the notion of there being a connection between scientific theories: theories based on the works of Einstein, Sir Isaac Newton, Charles Darwin, and more recently Stephen Hawking, and most germane to RV, Werner and Birgit Loewenstein, who have shown that every cell in our body sends and receives information constantly.[81] Psychic experiences steeped in intuition and extrasensory abilities are validated now, although they have never seemed ridiculous to me. Any attempt to disprove such seemed pointless because all things are made of atoms which are the basic building block of ordinary matter, and matter is anything that can be touched physically. Everything in the Universe is made of matter and you can think of matter as microscopic books of DNA,[82] possessing the history of the humble beginnings of all things. All things are made from the same atomic source.

Then, there is energy. What is that made of?

Physicists determined that atoms are made up of vortices of energy constantly spinning and vibrating, radiating with their own unique energy signature. All things have their own signature, meaning that no two can ever truly be considered alike. Just like fingerprints or snowflakes, no two are identical. We **are** beings of energy and vibration, radiating our own unique signature.[83] Energy is the measure of matter's motion. Even thought is comprised of energy, and is thought to have the potential to travel faster than the speed of light.[84]

When using psychometric techniques to measure the energies of a person or thing, our sensory body is essentially reading or decoding the spinning, vibrating, radiating energy signatures in order to understand the energy we have encountered. Where did that thing come from? What history is held within its atomic structure? What does it like or dislike and what other connections does it possess? Such questions can all be answered by allowing oneself to remain open to the transference and cellular communication that occurs when we use our sensation of touch to unravel or decipher energy signatures.

When two electrons are close together, they will vibrate in unison. This is called Quantum entanglement. When separated, the two appear to be connected by an invisible thread or, rather, an umbilical cord emerges between them even if they are separated by many light years. When one of these electrons is jiggled, the other electron senses the vibration instantaneously and responds. Physicists call the influencing of electrons at a distance entanglement. Our thought is comprised of electrons. By merely thinking of someone or something with whom we have been entangled, we will influence them in some way. As a demonstration; (of the power of one electron within the process of thought) let us just imagine that an electron in one molecule hops on over to another electron filled molecule whereby they become entangled. That entanglement allows for the transference of information across a seemingly forbidden gap which is known as quantum tunneling.

A dancing or jiggling electron can be a tangible object and at the same time be an oscillation of energy.

Quantum mechanics holds that any given particle has a chance of being in a whole range of locations and… occupies all those places at once. Physicists describe quantum reality in an equation they call the wave function, which reflects all the potential ways a system can evolve. Until a scientist measure the system, a particle exists in its multitude of locations. But at the time of measurement, the particle has to choose just a single spot. At that point the probability narrows to a single outcome and the wave function collapses, sending ripples of certainty through space-time. Imposing certainty on one particle could alter the characteristics of any others it has been connected with even if those particles are light-years away.[85]

In the quantum realm events unfold—outcomes change, alterations change, characteristics are changed—at speeds that would be unachievable with classical physics alone, as touted by author Mark Anderson in "Discover, Science for the Curious." He says that quantum phenomena are seen in laboratory settings, in vacuum chambers chilled to near absolute zero, whereas biological systems are more notably warm and wet, filled with life noise that could potentially "drown out any quantum weirdness that could rear its head."

How does this Quantum Entanglement work in the real world?

If thought truly moves at speeds in excess of the speed of light, then information can be sent from the mind of one person to another at breakneck speeds with little effort. We can even think about something; let us use the racecar incident as an example; and all electrons associated with that racecar can in effect transfer information by means of quantum tunneling (as described previously). I don't totally understand everything there is to know about these occurrences, but I am showing you that there is an underlying methodology based in physics and a not a mystical force at work in and around our lives. I hope to dispel any mysticism associated with abilities such as mine. We can all perform acts such as these. It's naturally exciting to think about being a part of an elite club of extraordinary individuals who experience life in profound ways, but the facts speak for themselves. Scientists have documented how the quantum world works, but I sometimes wonder if they totally realize to what degree our vibrating bodies of energy can influence our environments? They say we all can, although not many can put the pieces together as I am doing for you now.

In my world, space and time hold little meaning. I think of something, or touch something and information is transferred from whatever it is I am focusing on and into the cells of my body to decipher. When an organ or system within the body is out of balance, vibrating or oscillating at a rate that is not healthy for the individual, my body realizes the imbalance and allows me to feel exactly what the individual is feeling. In this way, I entered the realm of remote healing.

Psychometry opened the portal

My very first, very real, very emotional experience with psychometry occurred in 1989, after I had moved to Florida and opened a cleaning business. The stress of the move, moving away from my family and opening the business, got to me, so I decided to take a meditation class. The woman who taught the class looked like the psychic medium in the Poltergeist movie played by Zelda Rubinstein. She was robust, confident, sensible and inviting, yet real. After my first class, something happened to me, inside of me. Whether it was the practice of deep breathing, the quieting of my mind, the realness of the instructor or the accretion of all factors, a seal was broken. I was immediately connected to the world in a way that I had never experienced before that first class.

One day after class the instructor asked me to stay. When all other attendees left she quietly pulled an envelope from her desk drawer and slowly handed me the closed, sealed envelope while looking deeply into my eyes. She said, "Nicole, you have a gift and I want to help you nurture it. I believe that your gift is so strong that you will be able to do amazing things with it and if you don't do good things, you could potentially do very bad things to yourself and others."

I felt a deep sigh escape from within me. She placed her hand on the envelope that now lay in my hands and said, "Please tell me what is in the envelope." With two hands I began to turn the envelope to the seam to open it. She quickly grabbed my hands and said no. That perplexed me. How was I going to tell her what was in the envelope without opening it? She touched my shoulder softly and reiterated that I possessed an incredible ability and that I would not have to open the envelope to tell her what was in it. She said that if I placed the envelope between my hands and closed my eyes, I would be able to 'see' the treasure sealed within.

Scared, I jumped from my seat and told her she was crazy. Her voice became deep and forceful, with a twinge of urgency vibrating within it. It gave me pause. I sat and did as she asked. As she walked me through the breathing exercises we had done in the meditation classes, I closed my eyes. She said that all I had to do is think of opening myself up to what was coming from within the envelope. I imagined opening my mind. With my physical eyes closed, I somehow opened my inner sight and a window or door into my brain unlocked. It looked as if a black screen had been placed before my brain and colors, objects, and swirling energy took the place of my normal physical eyesight. Still with eyes closed a picture began to form within my brain. I could see bright beautiful blue eyes, brown curly hair and dark skin. As I squinted inwardly, trying to make sense of what I was seeing. A full face came into clear view. What I saw was a picture of a handsome little boy of about 2 years in age with blue eyes, dark skin and dark curly hair. Intrigued by what had transpired, I trusted what I saw, so shared what I had seen with my instructor. She took a deep breath, threw her head back in relief and smiled as she motioned for me to open the envelope.

I remember opening that envelope very slowly, feeling as if that day, that exact moment would be one I would never forget. Somehow in the movement of breaking the seal on the envelope my life would never be the same. The feeling I had in that instance proved time and time again to be correct.

As the paper crackled between my fingers, I closed my eyes, split the two sides of paper and reached in to touch its contents.

When firmly in my hand, I opened my eyes and what I saw was nothing short of amazing. The exact picture I saw in my mind's eye lay in my hand.

Very matter-of-factly, the instructor said, "Now tell me where he is." More scared than before, I leapt out of my seat, heading for the door. Again, I told her she was crazy. Not only would I not do it, I could not do it. I am not sure where the fear came from, but for some reason I felt a very real threat existed by opening myself up in this way. She reacted to my fear by snatching me by the shirt and forcibly pulling me back to sit down next to her.

My mind raced, making me wonder what the urgency was about and in that instant my fear subsided and my empathy kicked in. She was scared. She was fearful. Not for herself but for the boy in the picture. Coming to this realization was transformational. Something within me understood that this was not about me. It was about the boy. I could feel that she needed my help.

As I experienced my epiphany, she noticed my shift. It felt like my brain had expanded; it was thick but open, deep, malleable and ready to receive more. Then something in my body snapped. It was as if all the cells within me came alive. Imagine trillions of cells that look like the Pacman men within the Pacman computer game all standing at attention, looking up toward the brain, waiting for further instructions.

The instructor told me that she and a dear friend, who was at that time an ex-CIA agent, were working on a closed "missing person" case. This child was two when he disappeared and it had been eight years since the case went cold. She had tried to communicate with his energy, thinking and feeling as if he had died, but she kept hitting a dead end. She went on to say that she knew when we first met that I was to help her and, now that I had calmed my own internal chatter, I was ready to learn how to do this.

She had me hold the picture within my hands and go back to my deep breathing. I closed my eyes and the child's face came back into my inner mind's view. I imagined that I was plugging myself into his energy like one would do by plugging a light cord into an electrical box. The child came to life and it was as if I was inside of him. His body lay on the back seat of his fathers' car. As if we were one, he and I looked up and out of the car window, watching the trees swish by. Our heart was beating slowly and it felt as if we were getting cold even though we were wrapped in a blanket. We lay motionless and peaceful, taking in the tree tops and road signs as they went by. The car stopped and the father climbed out from behind the wheel. He opened the back door and tugged at the blanket, pulling us into his arms. He carried us for some distance through a wooded area. I could smell the dank soil. The woods were filled with dogwood trees and the area seemed very familiar to me.

In that instant, a memory surfaced that had been stored within the cells of my body. In the memory, I was a thirteen year old child hiking the Virginia woodlands with my dear friend and her sister. Her sister had been doing field research to get her Veterinary degree, and my bestie and I had gone down to visit to help her collect specimens (worms, spiders and such.) My brain linked the smells and the predominant dogwoods to this exact area. As my cells made the connection, I was transported back to the child being carried by his father. Now, not connected as one, I could walk beside them to take in the environment. As we walked, there were spirits dressed in civil war garb running around shooting at each other. They were not physically there, but energetically tied to this area somehow. I took note and started to connect the dots. Then, a field of green filled my mind's eye and a cartoon character began running through this field. That disappeared and a two by four piece of wood appeared for my viewing, and it swung down out of the sky aiming straight for my head. It felt so real, I actually ducked, and the instructor asked me to describe what I was seeing. I relayed the information, but it made no sense to her, so I went back to what the child was showing me.

An object appeared which look like a triangle, then another object, this one being a circle. The circle lay before a small hill and the triangle lay flat on the ground, as if each was communicating with me. The circle formed more circles looping and running back into the hillside. The triangle embedded hundreds more triangles and ran deep into the earth. My brain and body cells starting piecing the information together and without consciously helping, the storyline came to life.

The green field, the man running in that field of green, and the two-by-four became "Mine Run, Virginia," and the "Greenwood Mine," also in Virginia. I made mental notes and went back to paying attention to the data that was streaming in.

I was pulled high into the sky so that I could survey the area. I could see the roadways and how they intersected. A major roadway intersected into a Y formation and the words Mine Run and Paytez or Payne floated through my mind. I was drawn then to move back down to the boy and his father. The father placed him on the ground. He was covered in a blanket and I watched as the boy's final resting place was dug. I looked back at the boy and his body became an outline of energy. His throat area lit up as if highlighted by a thin white vibratory light. I watched helplessly as his energy slipped away. He died that day, laying there in the dank dark soil with Spirits from the Civil War re-enacting a deadly power struggle. There was a sense of resolve emanating from him; his father loved him and there was nothing he could do to change what had happened.

I stood quickly as the information coursed through my veins and I walked to the door. My instructor asked me where I was going. I said goodbye, hollering back over my shoulder with a perplexed grin on my face, "I will be back. I've got to go look for something."

Not really sure where I was going or what I was looking for, I got into my car and sped off in search of a local library. I found one between my instructor's home and my own. As I walked through the door, something told me to use the computer to plug in some of the information I had received. Dogwood trees of Virginia, Mine Run, Greenwood mine, Military bases of Virginia, and Wars of Virginia. I accumulated a pile of books and looked inside them, still not clear on what I was looking for. I found a number of things that sort of fit. I made copies of the pages to take them home so I could meditate on what had been handed to me. I remember feeling a bit overwhelmed, exhilarated, and yet beaten until I reached the end of the last book on the table. There it was. A sign! Something I could not dismiss. It felt like the Universe was calling me out. *Mineral Resources, Virgina,* it read, in black print, with its address and phone number clearly listed in dark bolded print, jumping off of the page.

I headed home. Once settled back in at home, I dialed the number. The phone rang and a deep masculine voice answered. "Good afternoon, Division of Geology and Mineral Resources, this is Michael Upchurch."

I took a deep breath, "Hello Michael, my name is Nicole and this is going to be a very odd conversation. If you will bear with me I will explain."

His voice softened and sounded as if he had the patience of a saint. "Sure Nicole. How can I help you?"

"Well Michael, I have recently been introduced to the world of psychic phenomenon [the known and identifiable term at that time of my life] and my instructor involved me in a missing persons case where a child disappeared eight years ago. I have never done this sort of thing before and, quite frankly, I am searching for proof that I did in fact make contact with a child I have never met. As my instructor guided me into a trance-like state, I saw some things in my mind's eye. I don't know if you believe in this sort of thing but I hope you can help me. Would you mind if I share what I saw so that I can figure out whether these places exist or not?"

"Yes, Nicole. I have just the thing that can help us; it's a computer that links me to the entire area. As you tell me what you saw I can plug in words and we will see what comes up."

I ran through all of the things I had seen while being connected to the missing child. Michael's computer proved to be a Godsend.

"Nicole, we have a Mine Run and we have two Greenwood mines. One runs back into a hillside and the other runs straight down into the earth."

You can imagine my surprise. "I saw spirits of men running around hiding behind trees and rocks, shooting at one another. Did a war or battle take place there?"

"Yes, one took place nearby."

"Is there a military base nearby? As the child and I were linked together I could hear planes flying over, but they were not normal commercial planes. They sounded like heavy military planes."

'Yes, there is," he said.

"Michael, are there any maps of the area and if so, can I get one?"

"Sure, I can actually blow up the maps, print them out and FedEx them overnight to you so that you and your people have them in the morning Nicole."

I thanked him for listening and for his willingness to help and we hung up.

This experience rocked my world. I was amazed at the clarity of the information and still even more amazed that Michael could tap into a computer that would provide us with proof that this place actually existed. I had never physically been to the location where the child took me but I had been to the Virginia woodlands. The place was stored within the cells of my body right down to the smell of the soil and the genre of trees that were indigenous to that specific area. What would have happened had I doubted any of those things I had seen and experienced?

The next morning I opened the package. Maps! Each map showed the area in question, with another blown up bigger to get us closer to the mine and the roadway where the father drove to bury his son in a secluded spot. I circled the spot between the road and the Greenwood mine that ran straight down into the earth, bound the maps with rubber bands, and drove to my instructor's home.

My heart was racing as I knocked on her door.

"Well, did you find anything?" she asked.

I handed her the maps.

"I have circled the exact location where the child took me."

She opened the maps on the kitchen table and I pointed to where the circle was.

"How did you do this?" she inquired.

I told her and said, "I am sure you can imagine how scared I was to call the number and how amazed I was to find out that the place with all of the descriptors was real." She hugged me and reiterated that it was important that I use my new found gift to do good things.

That was the beginning of an amazing journey. Each technique I learned, each client I worked on, each project, allowed me to practice and hone my skills. With practice, I gained more confidence and I found new and better ways of managing my abilities and doing incredible things.

Interestingly, you don't have to have first-hand knowledge or an education in a particular field to trust the information that comes through intuitively. You can trust the information you get intuitively, and then use the internet or an encyclopedia to confirm it. By being open and willing, the Universe conspires to help you and then you attract more data. Being the detective and doing our follow up research on specific words is easy.

I will share an example. When I was looking up the information about Mineral Resources, I read, "The Mine Run Campaign; The Battle of Mine Run ran from November 27th through December 2nd of 1863 in Orange County Virginia with an inconclusive outcome between Commanders Major General George Meade of the Army of the Potomac and General Robert E. Lee of the Army of Northern Virginia." Finding that information confirms my trust in the Universe and how we communicate with one another. Finding such validation simply amazes me, even now after all of these years.

As I learned more about the process, there appeared to be many uses for this skillset. I jumped at every chance I got to touch and extract information from whatever I could get my hands on. Touching a tree made me feel as if bugs were crawling all over me and when the wind was blowing I felt as if I was swaying in the exact same way the tree was. Touch a dog and I could see through its eyes, see what it looked at, who it liked, didn't like, how it ate, where it liked to go, and so on. Touch a newly trained yearling and watch it win its first professional horse race. Touch a human and see through layers of flesh and bone; feel its sorrows and joys. Touch a race car and, well, you get my point. There seemed to be no end to what one could look at or see into by using the technique.

As amazing as it felt, I just had to know how I was able to experience such things. It wasn't enough to simply say I was psychic or intuitive. I had to know there was a scientific basis for such abilities, for myself to know, and so that other people wouldn't be afraid of it and potentially realize their own power.

At that time in my life, extraneous to my psychic abilities, it became necessary to hire an attorney to help me protect a patent I was working on. My attorney's son was experiencing severe vomiting episodes following a surgery to repair his esophagus right after birth. After much care and medical assistance, the issue showed no signs of letting up. The medical profession allowed they could see no workable solutions.

When the attorney, Michael, and I met to talk business, he shared this ordeal, saying that he and his wife were worn out and feeling quite defeated. He was worried his son might die. Feeling his fear I offered to help. I prefaced my offer by saying that I wasn't sure what would come of it, but that I was willing to try.

I met Michael and his wife at their home. I suggested he hold his son on his lap to help him feel safe, since he did not know me. I placed my right hand on his chest and my left hand on his back. I closed my eyes and relaxed. Almost immediately, I felt pressure building within my gut. My stomach became uneasy, as if I was getting ready to vomit. I watched the scene unfold as the acid moved up and out of the little guy's gut, burning his esophagus. My body took on his physical mannerisms as well as his emotional state; I felt listless and scared as the pressure built in my abdomen just before an explosive-like feeling gripped my chest. I watched as the cells of the boy's body showed me event after event where the blood and stomach acid flooded upward and out of his body. Other fluids and food particles not passable via the mouth found an alternate route out of the body by running through the digestive tract and out through the anus. As that scene faded within my mind's eye, I transported to a more specific area of his body. There I was standing upon the boy's diaphragm; just above what appeared to be a hiatal hernia; looking up into the esophageal tube. The tissue looked soft, but red and inflamed. I kept trying to look down towards the stomach but something kept nudging me to look back up into the esophagus. As I watched, a complex web of veins appeared and then all but one disappeared. The one that remained began to fill with blood like a balloon being filled with water. The ballooning vein reached max capacity and a tear or fissure formed in the esophageal wall allowing the hot bloody liquid to pour down past where I stood on the boy's diaphragm. As I sat with my hands on the lad I held one question in my mind, "What trigged the event?" As if hearing my thoughts, his body answered my question by showing me that the events were brought on by what the boy was ingesting. Whatever it was, it was continually irritating and inflaming the tissue, exacerbating the situation.

Once done viewing what his body wanted to show me, I asked for permission to share the experience with a friend in the medical professional.

My friend and I documented what transpired, illustrating on paper what the boy was going through in a way that his doctor could understand. The parents then shared it with their family doctor. Based on our findings the boy's physician pulled all medications, one of which was causing the ballooning. The father told me months later that his son vomited once more a week after his doctor pulled his meds, then all bloody episodes ceased. That was my first experience with healing.

There were many more, all a wonderful surprise to me to have orchestrated.

Distance Healing

Earlier, I described how, when an electron is jiggled, the other electron senses the vibration instantaneously and responds. This influencing of electrons at a distance is known as entanglement (referenced above). What makes this important to reiterate here, is the part about our thoughts being comprised of electrons, and when one electron in a molecule hops on over to another electron-filled molecule they become entangled. That entanglement allows for the transference of information across a forbidden gap and those electrons become one with each other. So entanglement is how healing at a distance can happen. When the healthy cells of one body enmesh with those of an unhealthy body the cells adjust to the higher vibratory rate. Not only did that infant's sick body react favorably to the removal of the medicine of insult, but it also received some of my own higher vibrations to start lifting it towards health.

Did I know this was going to happen when I first started doing remote healing? No, I didn't. Neither could I have predicted it would happen. As I streamed in information from clients, something strange happened. Each client would contact me to report that they were feeling different: better, more peaceful. They wondered what I was doing and whether I meant to heal them. Their pains were diminishing or completely gone. Although I had not provided them with an exact day and time that I would start or finish their session, they were in fact feeling something very different. This validates the action at a distance phenomenon, where intrinsic properties of one system induce a change in another, touting non-separability and holism.

I enjoyed using my healing ability. It felt good to help people and made me feel hopeful, as if with these gifts there was a divine order or reason for my being alive. I will be documenting many more of my remote healing experiences in books to come, as examples of how divine interventions can be obtained through us mortals.

I was enjoying my experiences, although there seemed to be no natural flow or order to them. Other people in my life were worried that I might burn myself out, and as I considered their concern I realized that there was a need to be more aware and purposeful with my abilities. If I were better able to channel my energy, I might be able to determine the source of the omnipotent energy that was at work in my life.

As I contemplated how to best use my energy I also had to consider how I had used my energy up to this point, which initiated this next event. Yes, I had done healing work, but I also have "saved" people, strangers, reaching out to the Universe for help.

Here is one example of an unexpected remote "save."

I was on an impossible mission to complete 50 tasks in one day, when normally I could manage, maximally, 14 of those same tasks in one long day. I decided to treat myself with a chai tea, to motivate me to get to work. As I pulled through a local Starbucks to make my purchase, I realized I spent a fair amount of time fixated on the things I thought I had to do each day. Not once had I ever prayed for direction or asked the Universe whether there was anything I could do to assist in the higher order of life. As that thought filled my head a new, more peaceful feeling entered my body. It felt as if my brain was expanding, triggering a portal to open at the top of my head to connect me to all life and the Universe. As I relished the newfound sensation, I noticed something, or maybe someone, was in the vehicle with me, although I couldn't see anyone. As if my voice was not my own, I spoke aloud in a way that felt foreign. "I spend each day thinking that I know best. I know I have many jobs to do today but for once I would like to see a higher power at work in my life. What can I do for you today?" Words that were not my own filled my head, offering specific instructions. It happened so quickly there was no way I could have made up such things.

"Drive nine miles north on route 29. There you will find a white car on the side of the road. Stop to speak to the woman in the car."

There was no doubt in my mind that 'something' or someone submitted the request. I asked for direction. I had never experienced anything like it before; so choosing how my day would go was my choice; I decided to go. I would get whatever jobs done that I was capable of doing after I followed the directions.

I set the trip meter and drove north on route 29. Imagine my surprise when I crested the top of the hill just before the nine mile mark and saw a white car sitting on the roadside. Goosebumps broke out all over my body. Thoughts raced through my mind as I got nervous about talking to whoever it was in the car. What do I say? Do I tell them what I was told to do? Do they need help? The same voice that instructed me put a stop to my inner chatter.

"Stop, just step out of the vehicle and ask her if she needs help!"

I pulled behind the car and noticed a woman leaning into the back fastening her children into their seats. I stepped out of the truck onto the running board and waved to her. She leaned out of her car to address me.

"Hello, are you okay? Can I help you with something?" I said.

"No, thank you. My sister had just dropped us back off to my vehicle after a short shopping trip and I was just getting the kids situated so we could head to the house."

"You're parked in a bad spot on a busy road," I said. "I am happy to wait until you get the kids situated."

"That is very sweet of you to want to do that, but I am almost done. I really appreciate you stopping. People don't do that anymore," she said with a heartfelt smile. "You can go on, we will be fine."

"Are you sure?" I said.

"Yes. Thank you."

As I began to pull away I noticed that she was crying. She waved at me to stop. "Yes, is something wrong?"

"I am not sure why I am telling you this, but this morning while praying I asked God to show me how much he loves me. I just realized that you brought me my answer."

With tears in my eyes, I whispered, "Yes, and you have no idea just how much." I waved goodbye and pulled away. I didn't know how to tell her what had just happened. Who would have thought?

The epilog to this story was that, strangely enough, I was able to complete 25 of the 50 tasks, a Herculean feat when 14 is the normal upper limit, and I believe that energy came because of the divine intervention of the emotional "save."

But it was not enough to do these saving things to others' emotions, illnesses, dangers. These experiences catapulted me into studying the science of the human body and its functions. It wasn't enough that my body could see, hear, smell, taste and feel what was going on inside of another, I had to know how to communicate with the doctors and patients in order to forge a clear line of communication so that they understood what was occurring when I received saving messages.

I have created methods and templates to RV the health, wellbeing and medical information of a client. Techniques associated with RV also allow me to "mind meld" with clients. Although I had been using psychometry to read the mind of clients who could not speak [Parkinson's, comatose, strokes, ALS, traumatic brain injury, etc.] in the past, RV took me one step further: it permitted me to stay unbiased.

In the beginning, while using psychometry to link-in to a client, I would so fiercely want for them to be well that my own perceptions and desires would taint the process. RV allows for the viewer to stay with the pure information, without trying to change it. It teaches us to trust what we sense.

I have heard other intuitive people talk about how their gifts were revealed to them only after they had suffered a near death experience or physical trauma. I had a number of traumatic experiences throughout my life, although I don't believe we have to suffer traumas to get in touch with this side of ourselves. When working with clients and their children I am able to teach them in minutes what took me years to learn on my own. Everyone is empathic to a certain degree. Everyone is born with extra sensory abilities, although during rearing most children are not taught to develop them. Adults don't always realize that the brain of a child is malleable and capable of absorbing massive amounts of information. With purposeful practice and using intuitive abilities, RV becomes second nature: an acquired behavior or trait. If we learn to trust what we sense at an early age, we can not only obviate or prevent illness, accidents and trauma. We can learn to live life more fully; engaged, awake, and in acceptance of the extraordinary power we all possess.

This is how science and spirituality work together. Thank you, Nicole, for sharing your experiences. We look forward to more of your work to guide us into remote viewing and healing.

It looks as if we all can learn her skills. What happens, though, when you can't receive and/or process light messages?

Chapter 11

When Intuition Can't Be Accessed

It was as a Special Educator that I began to puzzle how the brain knows in advance what it should do, and then I was given the answer to the puzzle: the brain is primed by light messages available to us through what we call "intuition."

Earlier, I was puzzling how an LD kid could know the right answer but give a wrong answer. Then, we saw what happens when you experience neuronal derailments: glitches, slips-of-the-tongue, word-finding problems—processing run amok so that wrong answers occur and sometimes "crazy," de-regulated thoughts happen. It's a neural-linkage schmozzle when the neuronal train derails. Sometimes the train can't be righted and is lost. Abandoned, as in "Uh, I forgot the question." Sometimes it does nothing but shunt into the wrong siding before starting again, disobeying its preafferent plan, only to shunt wrongly again, so we get false starts and hesitations. Some persistent non-calm, derailed mind states can prevent access to our intuition. For example:

ANXIOUS BRAIN,

BUSY BRAIN,

DAMAGED BRAIN,

DAYDREAMING BRAIN,

DEPRESSED BRAIN,

DRUGGED BRAIN,

FEARFUL BRAIN,

"i-MIND" BRAIN,

LOVESTRUCK BRAIN,

STRESSED OUT BRAIN,

TUNED OUT BRAIN,

WRONGLY WIRED BRAIN,

PRESSURED BRAIN,

and, in cases of anencephaly, MISSING BRAIN.

Some of these mind states can be temporary, while others are permanent or permanent until (miraculously) cured. Many of these mind states cause, or are caused by neuronal trains that loop or derail, instead of moving forward: stalling, staying in one place, or bouncing around from one rumination to another, missing the focused, alert, and calm state required to be OPEN to inuition.

Let's look at the mind state, for instance, of someone with Autism as they try to understand heard messages. Researchers have discovered that in most cases of Autism, the processing of individual sounds takes a fraction of a second longer than for people who don't have Autism. It isn't much of a delay for a neuronal train receiving the phonemes (that is, the speech sounds) from which it puts together a word, but the cumulative cascading effect of the time lag for sound recognition causes confusion and misunderatnding by the end of a whole sentence.[86] Because communication is so difficult for people with autism: we see autists struggle with the results of inability to understand long messages or commands originiating out-loud with autists' family members or teachers. So, we might not be surprised to imagine a near impossibility of listening to and understanding messages sent from the zero point field as well. In this, there might be no difference from the difficulties encountered in listening to and understanding messages that come from another person. We might sympathize with a struggle to bring order to chaos in a mind that doesn't attune to the messages fromlight.

Or, maybe not. Perhaps holographic messages are easier for autists, bypassing some of the disconnected entrainments? Maybe they can receive harmonic messages that go directly to the emotional centre of the brain. We know that dolphins communicate holographically, and being around dolphins has a magical "normalizing" effect on kids with Autism. Who knows? Maybe bypassing words is helpful in receiving light messages. But, I think it more likely that the messages become less clear if delayed by the same point four milliseconds suffered in processing speech sounds. While Autists often act impulsively, their actions do not always suggest that they are obeying messaages of beneficient intuition.

Unlike Autism, Learning Disabilities are more hidden and it takes a trained eye and an astute parent to see the problem when a kid has a correct intention, knows the answer and does the wrong thing (and not out of spite but out of sheer error). One would not automatically expect someone with LD to have difficulty learning to get into an Alpha mind state to receive beneficient messages from light. But, according to Swingle in her book, i-MINDS, getting into an Alpha state of meditative readiness is not automatic for people with LD, including ADHD, and sometime their brainwaves will look like they are going into an Alpha state but in fact their oscillations are spindling "absent," how seizures appear on a brain scan. Swingle warns that overexposure to the internet, particularly hours and hours spent on egames, can cause this dangerous spindling Alpha which affects the creativity and imigination part of the brain.[87] The visualization required for receiving holograms may be sluggish or absent.

In terms of seizures affecting message reception, there is at least one researcher who believes spiritual visions are nothing but temporal lobe seizures. Persinger at Lauretian University in Sudbury, Ontario uses what he calls the "God-helmet," the wearers of which demonstrate seizure activity when they are reporting spiritual events as they undergo assessment. He believes "cerebral fritzing is responsible for almost anything one might describe as paranormal—aliens, heavenly apparitions, past-life sensations, near-death experiences, awareness of the soul, you name it."[88] Rather than light messages affecting brain functions, Persinger attributes intuition directly to internally-generated changes in brainstates. But if that were the case, then people who have cerebral fritzing all the time, would be the most spiritual, calm, holy, and enlightened of us all. The opposite is more apparent: neural fritzing interferes with reception of messages. Fritzing derails the neuronal train.

Let's revisit derailing, and look a little deeper to illustrate what happens in a neuronal derailing:

Neuronal misfiring occurs when the messages in the brain cells do not hop from one cell to another in the way they are supposed to. Errors occur, often without the person knowing they have occurred.

One neuron (one brain cell) among billions in any brain can put the train at risk. Of the multiple places where synapsing with the next cell can go wrong, if that neuron fails to uptake into the train, there is a misfire. Whatever the preaffernt plan, a fritz or glitz, a mistiming, and the unintentional routing takes place. Incorrect thoughts and answers result.

Most people know this much about neurons: information contained within a cell nucleus is moved along by an electrical charge towards the receiving end of the next neuron, at the dendrites. In this next neuron, the charge collects/recognizes/interfaces with information stored inside this cell nucleus (in the centre of the cell body, which is where the DNA also is), before moving out along the axon to target a further gathering of information from the next neurons in the neuronal chain. This is called information processing. We process information whenever we think, do, perceive, or act.

At the point where messages have to jump from brain cell to brain cell (neuron to neuron), chemicals flood into the space between the cells, allowing the message to move across the gap and continue its electric charge along the next neuron. Of course, it should only be travelling there if that is the correct neuron along the planned preafferent path. That gap between the neurons is called the synapse, otherwise known as the junction between the axon of the sending cell and the dendrites' receptors on the receiving cell. The synapse is like the love two people have to feel before they marry and give everything to their significant other. It's the place where the chemical juices secrete to temporarily bond the two cells.

So the neuronal train has information moving along one cell to another cell, assisted by the synapses, and this is happening in multiple different sites before they all come together in a well-timed co-ordinated response across groups of cells. For example, to recognize the capital letter H, there is a neuron that recognizes the upright sticks, and another neuron that recognizes the horizontal dash between the sticks, so these two grapheme recognition cells must kickstart their recognition electrical charges, and then must synthesize to come up with the complete grapheme we call "H."

Charges move along axons towards the dendrites of the next cell. The information goes "out" along the axon, towards the next neuron.

The chemicals at the gap (at the synapse) are called neurochemicals. They are made up of proteins (enzymes) which our brain manufactures from the things we eat and drink. They are susceptible to insult. They will react nastily to being insulted. For instance, we all have seen how our chemical balance will be "off" in some way if we drive our blood sugar nuts by eating an entire tub of ice cream. You might have to get comatose for a few hours to let your chemicals recover from such insult.

There are plenty of examples of things that happen to us when our neurochemicals are insulted or sluggish, and these things have nothing to do with LD, but just happen to us. For example, slips of the tongue are significantly higher in women three days prior to menstruating, and an increase in men causing car accidents is associated with increase in their life-stress situations, and/or untreated depression. Mind states affect neurochemicals which, in turn, affect behavior. Sluggish brainwaves have a hard time responding to urgent demands.

Think of a chemical imbalance as the culprit in most neuronal train derailings. You can have LD, ADHD, Depression, Anxiety, sadness and daydreaming, or simply far too active neurons due to your nutritional habits or due to genetics of how your brain is wired, or an interaction of those things.

When synapses go awry in anyone's brain, LD or not, the receiving neuron may not fire up at precisely 0.4 milliseconds, which is the usual train speed in most stimulus-response effects. The neuron-messaging train will go speeding off onto tangents (spurs). It may get lost, as in "What was the question again?" Other times, however, the message will jump to a nearby (and therefore similar) track. Neurons group themselves in clusters of "like populations," so nearby clusters will have similar categories of information stored there. A response where the synapse has jumped to a nearby cluster, will be sort of related to the question, but will be inaccurate and sometimes make no sense at all, depending on the size of the jump.

Errors simply indicate typical neurochemical screw-ups, synaptic glitches, which hijack the thought off its track, or derail it completely. When we are tired, not in top form, hungover, grieving, or (strangely enough) over-excited and crazy happy, we all experience greater glitching. Derailments happen to everyone every once in a while, and to the person with LD, far too often.

Earlier, we discovered what happens if our neurons get in harmony with our messages: life runs smoothly, everyone benefits from harmony. So we know that the chances for being in harmony with the world of ideas are more limited for people with LD. They have to work much harder to hush, to calm their unquiet brain activity. Their trains are derailing a lot, particularly when they are stressing by trying so hard to focus. More than anything else, these derailings speak to the need to teach meditation to youngsters, particularly those with LD.

However, from firsthand experience teaching pre-teens and young teens to meditate, some students with ADHD appear unable, simply and totally unable to meditate, for they are unable to hold still and to quiet their brains for even a brief minute. Notably, these are students who choose not to use medication to stimulate their synapses into kicking in correctly, and nor are they helping their brainwaves with EEG mind state exercises. They have trains that bounce and bounce all over the place, all the time. It is very hard for them to focus at all, on anything that moves slower than they do, and focusing on quiet with the mindfulness needed to meditate is just not possible for them. Their neuronal trains keep chugging even when they try to shunt them into a station for a little while.

The benevolence bestowed in harmonic threads may not be apparent to ADHD sufferers when their neuronal trains continually misfire. A sense of rightfulness with the world may be not be available to them. The sureness that comes with accessing one's inner voice will be lost to them. The students who are most likely to be in "time out" are least likely to have tools available to calm and get ready to return to a quiet task. If they are to come to peaceful harmony with their light messages, all efforts to help them stop and listen to their messages should be explored. It is so important to assist this population in developing access to their intuition. This means, instead of sending them to time out, the class would benefit from taking frequent time out during lessons with the sole purpose of listening to one's inner voice: building the habit of mindfulness, so to speak. It is more than just a wistful hope for LD kids to be able to do this, for by calming the brain they will reduce their errors, and errors have a cumulatively terrible effect on attitude and emotions.

We explored preafference. Well *reafference* is what happens right after the glitches occur. In preafference, the sensory processors are primed to receive an anticipated sensation and if the signal comes in as expected, the mind reacts with an unconscious "all is well" emotional response. Reafference happens if the actual signal is different from what was expected. All glitched neuronal trains provide different-than-expected signals along the loop to the emotional centre of the brain, to the hippocampus and the amygdala within that. Right then, to compound the glitched information, when the limbic system (the emotions centre in the brain) gets involved, all sorts of negative emotions emerge to enter the conflict between the anticipation and the result – the result that went against the brain's PLAN. So the work of the brain gets much harder, not just reevaluating the input to correct the response, but also now to deal with an emotional onslaught that floods the brain with feelings relative to making errors. We've all had those feelings: those sinking feelings of disbelief and disappointment in ourselves. People with LD have them all the time, whenever their neuronal trains derail and they are aware of it. Loads of times. Every day.

When messages from light meet a terrible point of derailment, not only are the messages missed, the harmony is missed, and the negative emotions kick in. LD people who cannot access harmonic wisdom, feel crappy about themselves. They get no calmness, no sureness, no confidence in their choices. To them, they are always wrong. They call themselves "stupid."

How to help those with LD to access their intuition and guide them in their thoughts and responses?

There are some important assists beyond meditation that can help those with LD and ADHD get into a mind state receptive to intuition. Training in helping them learn how to control their own mind states is essential to be ready to access their intuition.

But, wait! People with LD are not the only ones who can't access their inner voice, who can't speak to the Universe and get good guidance. Lots of people try and try to ask the Universe for help, but fail to master meditation, even while longing to do both those things.

I have no idea which meditation methods are best from the list in Appendix A, because I haven't tried them all. I can make no recommendations of any one over another. But I have discovered the fastest way I know of getting into an Alpha mind state without meditating. Alpha is the bandwidth of electro-vibrations, the mind state which appears to be prerequisite to communicating with the energy field. It should come as no surprise to know that this method was shown to me by the Universe (I have come to expect no less guidance from Source).

The next and final chapter of this book describes the Alpha fast track.

Chapter 12

Fast Track To Alpha and Intuition Using EEG

ELECTRIC ENERGY ASSISTED by neurochemicals is how information gets moved along, or "processed," in the brain. The brain is an electrochemical organ (an oscillation machine) using electromagnetic energy to function. We can tell how well or poorly that energy is generating in a brain by measuring the waves the energy puts out.

The easiest way to measure those waves is with an EEG machine (an electroencephalogram) to capture and show a person's brain energy in real time. Electrical activity emanating from the brain is displayed in the form of brainwaves on the EEG screen, so we can see our own brain's activity, our own mind states.

All of us experience different kinds of brainwaves throughout the day: fast ones, slower ones, spikes, spindles, flat bits, irregular patterns, as well as nice regular rhythm ones. The brain chatters away all the time. The speed and amplitude of our electrical activity varies enormously, depending on situation, task, setting, neurochemical balance, bodily state, and emotions. Neurons constantly light up in all different parts of the brain. Those who say we only use something like 10% of our brains at any time – meaning, with help (usually their help) you can learn to use more – they don't seem to know that 100% of the brain actually works out most of the time (except in injured parts). If you look at brainwave activity on any scan machine, at any time, you will see that brainwaves constantly move up and down and across the brain, even sideways then up or down, and they also fire up (albeit much more slowly) when we are asleep. It would be hard to say which neurons are not getting a little electrical exercise in any given day. All parts of our brains are busy, primed and ready to be pulled by preafference into a neuronal train.

However, when we sample the brain's electrical activity, we don't see all of it at once. Depending on where we place the contact electrodes onto the scalp, we will see a dominant electrical wave stronger than the rest of them, AT THAT SAMPLE MOMENT. What we are seeing is your brain's current favourite range of oscillating energy which is at this time overriding the other waves. We can see if you are ruminating, worried, or alert: poised to problem solve, or to daydream, or to be confused, or calm. We can tell these mind states by measuring the cycles per second (which we name the Hz) of your brainwaves. Remember, they are waves, so they repeat in a rhythmical pattern, just like waves in the ocean.

The hertz measurement of electrical brainwaves is a unit of measurement of the frequency of a brainwave, better described as how often the wave waves. A frequency of 1 hertz means that something happens once a second. In brainwave territory, that's really slow. Charged-up neural oscillations go faster, definitely more than one cycle per second. If your brain waves are only waving once in that second, you are probably asleep or comatose, in fact, you are practically at the zero cycle per second reading which is how our brainwaves read on an EEG when we are quite dead. Alert brains wave a lot faster.

The cheapest and longest-known, tried and true brainwave reader is the EEG (even those are not actually cheap, costing around $5,000.00, but that is relatively cheap compared to, say, an MRI or a PET scanner). You have probably seen this machine used in film clips as "lie detectors," with zig zags of spikes and dips recorded by a pen on a page of continuous feed paper. Nowadays, the computer screen replaces the pen and paper. The recording is a visual record of electrical brainwaves sensed by an encoder attached to the electrodes which are attached to the client. Just like on a lie detector, an EEG assessment and monitoring of brainwaves uses an encoder that translates the electrical energy signals from the person into visible waves on the screen. The EEG is the machine, and the output is an electroencephalograph: the now-isible realtime electrical activity in the client's brain.

Different states of arousal display as different waves on the screen, slow, medium or rapid displays of output energy measuring anywhere between 3 Hz per second up to about 60 Hz per second, although we normally stop looking with interest at anything above 30 Hz because anything faster than that presents as almost a flat line blurr. Above 30 the height of the wave becomes so foreshortened by the wave's speed that the brain is obviously in overdrive and not putting out normal frequency waves.

So what is normal for a brain to exude?

The main frequencies of the human EEG waves are[89]:

- **Delta**: has a frequency of 3 Hz or below. Highest in amplitude (tallest zig zags) and the slowest, these waves are seen as the dominant rhythm in infants and in adult sleep. If your brainwaves are cycling at 3 per second and you are still awake, there is something very wrong. A coma, perhaps?
- **Theta**: has a frequency of 3.5 to 7.5 Hz. These "slow activity" waves are normal in children up to 13 years and in adult sleep but abnormal in awake adults. Theta is a very positive mental state found in day dreaming, dreaming, creativity, deep meditation, paranormal phenomena, out of body experiences, ESP, shamanic journeys. It indicates "inward thinking".

- **Alpha**: has a frequency between 7.5 and 13 Hz. These are lovely, regular, sinusoidal waves like the rhythm of a gentle ocean, and they appear when we are in the NOW, in the moment, and when closing the eyes and relaxing (but not so deeply as to go into Theta's inward thinking). They disappear when opening the eyes to become alert by thinking, calculating, problem solving, paying outward attention and trying to make sense of what is happening in front of you. This is the major rhythm seen in normal relaxed adults. It is present during most of life especially after the thirteenth year. Alpha waves place the brain in states of relaxation, non-arousal, calming meditation, hypnosis. This is the calm, alert, focused state that works best when trying to communicate with Source. Alpha waves are stronger than others, so once you are in an Alpha state, they block out interfering waves of other states, like the interference of too much inward thinking of Theta, or of too much energy of Busy-brain Beta
- **Beta**: beta activity is "fast" activity, frequency of 14 Hz and higher. This is the dominant rhythm in those who are alert but problem solving (around 18 Hz), but when it gets higher, this shows brain anxiety – in Hz of low 20's. These waves signify extroversion, concentration on an external problem, logical thinking, active conversation. However, the higher up in the 20's, the more buzz-saw the EEG waves appear, the more they reflect rumination, anxiety, depression, beyond problem solving and into neuronal train looping.

Meditation is facilitated through being in a calm, alert and focused state of Alpha, or even with slower rhythms of a Theta state of inward-looking, daydream-like, not attending to anything external.

Knowing the states conducive to meditation could help one access one's intuition. To speak to Source, your inner voice, the

Universe, it seems best to go into Alpha, the state where only the NOW matters.

People who meditate all the time, like Tibetan monks, go into a deeper-than-Alpha state, all the way into deep Theta, where waves are always creative, characterized by feelings of inspiration and very spiritual. It is believed that this mental state allows you to act below the level of the conscious mind.[90] Most regular meditaters have Theta waves going on in one part of the brain at the same time as dominant Alpha waves in another part of the same brain.[91] However, you do not need to be a regular meditater and go into such deep mindwave states to access your intuition. Alpha is necessary and sufficient.

Whether in Theta or in Alpha, meditation is the quelling of the mind, bringing it into a state where intuition can be accessed, along with perhaps sacred, holy, blessed, but definitely insightful information, definitely enlightenment and just daily intuition insights to guide you towards goodness. These relatively slow, calm brainwaves facilitate the opening of the portals to intuitions sent to us from another plane. You can think of meditation as mystical, for it is, but also as scientific, because meditation and brain chemistry allow self-regulation of brainwaves so that Alpha is dominant.

We all have random insights from our intuition, where we don't deliberately prepare or get into specific mindstates, but for those who want regular and practiced access to intuition, meditation is the way to master it. However, those who meditate to improve access to intuition say that it takes time to learn how to meditate. It takes effort and self-discipline, as well as a quiet space, to learn how to calm your brainwaves. How much time? Days? Months? Not everybody has that time (nor the ability, if they have a Busy Brain or a Rumination Brain problem). We have seen what happens to those with ADHD or LD: learning how to meditate can be a formidable task.

I discovered a way to get someone into Alpha quickly and reliably, even if they have a mind state dominance that outperforms their strong Alpha. This method works to overcome that. I call this method Mind Phasing (see www.mindphasing.com for photos and equipment). Busy brain, daydreaming, depressing ruminations, tangential ideas, defeatist feelings — these are all reduced as Alpha waves increase and block them. The more control you have over the NOW, which is the Alpha state, the less you are besieged by doubts, fears, worries, off-topic ideas, cynicism, and then the more you can seek guidance from the energy of the Universe, which wants you to be happy.

Using a dual-person EEG screen, where two people can be hooked up via electrodes and observe their brainwaves on the same screen, a novice meditator quickly entrains to the same brainwaves as the Alpha Entrainment Coach. Their oscillating energies rapidly phase with each other's.

In other words, I discovered that a seasoned meditater who easily gets themselves into an Alpha state, can sit beside the non-meditater; and when they both hook up electrodes on the scalp which read their brainwaves onto a monitor screen, and using the neurofeedback prompts on the screen, the Coach can coach the visible brainwaves of the partner, until those waves match the Entrainment Coach's Alpha waves.

It usually takes about five to 15 minutes for the novice to train their brain when they can see the waves on the screen and hear the prompts of bells ringing and lights flashing, whenever they make a match "hit" with the Coach. That is the beauty of EEG neurofeedback. The brain automatically wants to do again that which pleases it. In this case, it wants to do again that which brought the bonding of you to the other person through phasing your brainwaves. At most, it takes about 20 minutes, and so far, this method has never failed a novice to get into Alpha in the first session.

Furthermore, 80% of novices, once in Alpha, are able to ask the Universe their big "life questions": things like, "How can I manage my independence in my increasing old age? What is my true purpose in life?" Some people keep their questions private, but report receiving satisfactory answers. About 30% of successful Alpha clients wish to see or speak with a person who has passed away, and report (through their tears) that they were successful.

Since intuition not only gives wise advice about how better to say something, how better to act in certain situations, how better to consider someone else's motives, some clients enjoy using their new-found access to a spirit guide to ask those sorts of "how can I be a better person?" questions.

At this time, we are experimenting with bringing four or five different people into Alpha phase with each other using EEG headbands, where the mob of them will wear a new-EEG technology headband attached to their computers, sharing their brainwaves with others to quickly pull each other into Alpha. Just as those fireflies beamed in unison, the people in these experiments should oscillate in unison, for a feeling of connectedness and harmony with each other, to find common ground in their conjoint life purpose. Or, just to see how it feels to resonate coherently with others.

The Universe's guidance is about the will to harmony to make the world a better place. We all have a personal blueprint available from intuition for our divine purpose: something the world needs from us. Using EEG technology, we can improve our chances of working together on our divine purpose.

A few clients have asked about their genetic blueprint, when heritability factors point to danger from brain aneurisms, heart attacks, and the like. The Universe has responded to them with their life mission, the thing they should be doing because it is unique to their talents and experience and will give them tremendous satisfaction. The Universe usually suggests to follow our real life's purpose now, as shown by spirit guides, while we still can.

By learning to get into Alpha, even those whose brains put up barriers to meditative brainwaves can learn their life's purpose. It should be noted, however, that Alpha is not a simple mind state to get into for some. People who measure high for Alpha may in fact be spindling epilepsy or catatonia waves.[92] Those unable to consistently train to Alpha may want to have a thorough assessment through an MD referral to a Neurologist, because "when Alpha is not well-regulated , neither are you."[93]

As you can imagine, whenever any clients access the Universe for the first time by getting pulled into Alpha with an entrainment coach, or with others who can see their Alpha waves on a screen, they can be overwhelmed by their power to access a higher intelligence, the energy beyond us. Many cry grateful tears. Once in the habit of accessing their own intuition, they are candidates to use that access for any enlightened purpose, helping others as well as themselves, doing remote viewing, going forth to change the world for the better. It's all open once it's open.

If you don't have access to EEG headsets, hang out with someone who is habitually calm, focused and alert. That is a person most often in Alpha. Their waves are stronger than yours. Once you are calm, yourself, ask the Universe your questions.

Messages from light want to reach us. They are there for us. Whatever method works to get in touch with them, take it. Even if you never get a FLASH! the Universe always has something beneficial to say to you. You are beloved.

That was the vision brought to me by a stranger.

ENDNOTES

1. Wright, Simone. *First Intelligence: Using the Science and Spirit of Intuition,* (California: New World Library), 2014.
2. Nierenberg, Cari, "The Science of Intuition: How to measure 'Hunches' and 'Gut Feelings'," *Live Science.* Accessed May 2016. www.livescience.com/54825-scientists-measure-intuition.html.
3. Ibid.
4. Mossbridge et al, "Predictive Physiological Anticipation Preceeding Seemingly Unpredictable Stimuli: A meta-analysis, Frontiers in Psychology," *Frontiers in Psychology.* Accessed 17 October 2012, www.doi.org/10.3389/fpsyg.2012.00390.
5. Spottiswoode and May, "Skin Conductance Prestimulus Response: Analyses, Artifacts, and a Pilot Study." *Journal of Scientific Exploration,* 17(4), (December 2003): 617-641.
6. Gersten, Dennis. *Are You Getting Enlightened or Losing Your Mind?: A Spiritual Program for Mental Health* (New York, Harmony/Crown Books), 1997.
7. An index of famous people's biographies is available from O'Connor, J.J. and Robertson, E.F. This reference gives access to Pythagoras' story. www-history.mcs.st-and.ac.uk/Biographies/Pythagoras.html.
8. There are many versions of the life of Buddha. This is one: www.aboutbuddha.org/.
9. Readers can refer to a short account of Muhammad's life and work here: abuhaibeh.tripod.com/islam/muhammed.htm.
10. For biographical information on Hildegard of Bingham gathered from primary sources, see *Scivias,* www.pbs.org/wgbh/pages/frontline/shows/apocalypse.
11. Gersten, *Are You Getting Enlightened or Losing Your Mind?,* 3.

12. More on Hildegard, in German, from Holzinger, Regina. www.hildegard-frankfurt.info/index.php?option=com_content&view=article&id=46&lang=en.
13. The naturopathic route first propounded by Hildegard of Bingen: Hersch, Julie K. *Struck by Living*. www.struckbyliving.com/content/know-yourself-a-message-from-hildegard-von-bingen.
14. More information on Julian of Norwich is available in *Revelations of Divine Love*. www.pbs.org/wgbh/pages/frontline/shows/apocalypse.
15. Leech, Oliver, in his essay "The Mind-Body Problem," explains the three responses to the problem of defining what "*me*" really is: materialism, dualism and idealism. Dualism is the doctrine that physical things and mental states are both real but totally distinct and separate entities. www.philosophypathways.com/essays/leech1.html.
16. A grand tour of the mind/brain controversy, including Reductionism, Dualism, Functionalism, and Supervenience, is found in a 2011 essay by Laura Weed, "Philosophy of Mind: An Overview." Accessed Aug 2013: philosophynow.org/issues/87/Philosophy_of_Mind_An_Overview.
17. Emoto, Masaru, see ice crystals influenced by love and hate on Emoto's website. www.masaru-emoto.net/english/
18. Vaillant, George in "Positive Psychology and Love: Relationships and Wellbeing" *The British Psychological Society,* beta.bps.org.uk/events/positive-psychology-and-love-relationships-and-wellbeing.
19. Gersten, *Are You Getting Enlightened or Losing Your Mind?*, 3.
20. "In believing that creation followed a cosmic catastrophe and a fall of spiritual beings into matter... Blake believed his own visions, which included...sometimes a sense of cosmic oneness." Friedlander, E. *Understanding William Blake's "The Tyger"* (paragraph 5) www.pathguy.com/tyger.htm.
21. Tesla, Nikola, in "The Universal Energy of Vibrations," *Reflection Magazine*, Issue No.9, July/August 1998, 22. www.bibliotecapleyades.net/ciencia/esp_ciencia_universalenergy01.htm.
22. Nicolescu, B. in Needleman, J. and Baker, G. (eds.) *Gurdjieff,* (New York: Continuum International Publishing Group, 2004), 39.
23. Loewi, Otto, Nobel Lecture, Dec. 12, 1936, "The Chemical Transmission of Nerve Action." www.nobelprize.org/nobel_prizes/medicine/laureates/1936/loewi-lecture.html
24. Steven Strogatz, *Sync: The Emerging Science of Spontaneous Order.* (New York: Hyperion Theia, 2003), 61-2.
25. Samanta-Laughton, M. *Punk Science: Inside the Mind of God.* (O Books, 2006). Also, in an article entitled "Black Holes," Dr.

Samanta-Loughton says, "One of [black holes] more bizarre characteristics is that they periodically emit jets of very fast moving electrons, so fast that initially they appeared to be breaking the light barrier... Furthermore, the jets are emitted in a narrow beam, which is proving difficult to explain." However, those narrow beams may turn out to be the way information is sent from black holes. Dr. Manjir Samanta-Loughton, para 3, www.johnhuntpublishing.com/blogs/non-fiction/black-holes-by-dr-manjir-samanta-loughton/.

26. Haramein's lifelong vision of applied unified physics to create positive change in the world today is reflected in the mission of The Resonance Project Foundation, which he founded (it's all about resonating vibrational frequencies). www.facebook.com/Nassim.Haramein.official/posts/theres-is-a-fundamental-field-of-information-that-is-the-source-of-our-conscious/444557327; www.modernknowledge.ca/nassim-haramein-bio.html.

27. N,N-Dimethyltryptamine (DMT or N,N-DMT) can be consumed as a powerful psychedelic drug and has historically been prepared by various cultures for ritual purposes, to enter into the realm of the spirit. en.wikipedia.org/wiki/N,N-Dimethyltryptamine.

28. McCraty, Atkinson, and Bradley, "Electrophysiological Evidence Intuition: Part 1. The Surprising Role of the Heart." 2004. www.care2.com/greenliving/developing-your-hearts-intuition-3-quick-tips

29. Ibid.

30. Mysoor, Alexandra quotes Dr. Judith Orloff's contention that the entire right side of the brain is involved in intuition, in her article published in FORBES, called "The Science Behind Intuition and How You Can Use it To Get Ahead At Work." www.drjudithorloff.com/the-science-behind-intuition/. However, there is no citation provided, and no response to a query with Mysoor nor Orloff about that source.

31. McCrea, Siman M. "Intuition, insight, and the right hemisphere: Emergence of higher sociocognitive functions," *Psychol Res Behav Manag*. Published online Mar 2010 3: 1–39. McCrea supports a top down flow of insight.

32. Luo and Niki, "Function of Hippocampus in 'Insight' of Problem Solving," *National Institute of Advanced Industrial Science and Technology HIPPOCAMPUS* 13 (2003): 316 –323. doi.org/10.1002/hipo.10069

33. Wright, Simone. *First Intelligence: Using the Science and Spirit of Intuition.* (California: New World Library, 2014).
34. Ibid.
35. McCraty, Atkinson and Bradley "Electrophysiological Evidence of Intuition: Part 1 and Part 2," J Altern Complement Med. 10(2) (2004 Feb):133-43.
36. Haramein, Nassim, "Cognos 2010 Videotaped presentation in English, Part 2 of 6." *Pandoras Box.* Disappearing and reappearing discussion starts at 22:00 min. www.youtube.com/watch?v=aaJSPgBbUIs.
37. Ibid.
38. "'Sound and Light' explained in Great Detail," *Blunt Headed.* Sunday, December 28, 2014. In the hierarchy of vibrations, Sound and Light are below the subatomic, and at the sub-photonic level, right above the First Source which is at the level of Anti Matter. www.bluntaday.com/2014/12/sound-and-light-explained-in-great.html.
39. Moscowitz, Clara, "8 Shocking Things we Learned from Stephen Hawking's Book," *Live Science,* Jan. 2012, All about String Theory. www.livescience.com/18035-stephen-hawking-book-physics.html.
40. Schwabel, Herbert and Klima, Herbert. Spontaneous Ultraweak Photon Emission from Biologocal Systems and the Endogenous Light Field." *Forsch Komplementarmed Naturheilkd:* 2005; 12(2):84-9. Accessed on PubMed.gov: www.ncbi.nlm.nih.gov/pubmed/15947466.
41. The actual text...from *The Emerald Tablet of Hermes Trismegistus*, is: "That which is Below corresponds to that which is Above, and that which is Above corresponds to that which is Below, to accomplish the miracle of the One Thing." Thus, whatever happens on any level of reality (physical, emotional, or mental) also happens on every other level. The entry, *"As above, so below"* is in the article on Hermeticism, based on the teachings of Hermes Trismegistus, where God is unitary and transcendent and exits apart from the material cosmos. *en.wikipedia.org/wiki/Hermeticism.*
42. Further explanation: "Heart Hologramming – a practice in which an individual sincerely focuses/directs spirit and heart intelligence to the heart's true intent – likened to a hologram – to actualize it." Para 2. www.heartmath.org/articles-of-the-heart/heartmath-tools-techniques/heart-hologramming-want/.
43. Ji, Sayer "Biophotons: The Human Body Emits, Communicates with, and is Made from Light"; Biophotons are emitted by the human body, can be released through mental intention, and may

modulate fundamental processes within cell-to-cell communication and DNA: *GreenMed Info:* www.greenmedinfo.com/blog/biophotons-human-body-emits-communicates-and-made-light.
44. Brown, William, "The Light Encoded DNA Filament and Biomolecular Quantum Communication," originally published in *Nexus Magazine*, Vol. 19, No. 2, now on www.williambrownscienceoflife.com. *Morphic Resonance and Quantum Biology,* February-March 2012.
45. Ibid., 10.
46. Ibid., 4.
47. Ibid., 5.
48. Talbot, Michael. "*The Holographic Universe*" (New York: HarperCollins, 1991).
49. Sutherland, Mary, "*The Holographic Universe...and Our Spiritual Evolution*" 2006. www.bibliotecapleyades.net/ciencia/ciencia_holouniverse06.htm.
50. Miller, Iona "Wave Genetics: Wave Biology Beyond Molecular Genetics," *Holographic Archetypes,* 2013. www.holographicarchetypes.weebly.com/wave-genetics.html.
51. Garyaev, Dr. Peter "Diagnostic US Harms DNA." www.youtube.com/watch?v=G45hsWanB-A.
52. "In the yet-to-be-discovered science of multidimensional reality, waveforms can be sculpted to enter biogenetic fields and catalyze biochemical processes, restore cellular health and trigger encoded electromagnetic fields within the cellular functions of the Central Nervous System (CNS)." *Bluntheaded*: www.bluntaday.com/2014/12/sound-and-light-explained-in-great.html.
53. Miller, Iona and Richard Miller, "From Helix to Hologram, An Ode on the Human Genome" *Nexus,* Vol. 10.
54. Ibid.
55. Mahu, James. *Coherence of the Evolutionary Consciousness.* www.web.archive.org/web/20121017075151/http://wingmakers.com/music-hakomi4-6.html.
56. Sayer, Ji, "Biophotons: The Human Body Emits, Communicates with, and is Made from Light," *GreenMedInfo*: www.greenmedinfo.com/blog/biophotons-human-body-emits-communicates-and-made-light.
57 Grinberg, Dr. Jacobo, "Researcher of consciousness mysteriously disappeared," By News Center *Jewish Journal,* Accessed Mar 10, 2014: diariojudio.com/comunidad-judia-mexico/dr-jacobo-grinberg-investigador-de-la-conciencia-desaparecido-misteriosamente/15800/.

58. Black, Dr. Ira B. *"Information in the Brain,"* (Cambridge: MIT Press, 1994), 33
59. Ibid.
60. Ibid, 34.
61. Freeman, Walter J. *"How Brains Make Up Their Minds"* (New Haven: Phoenix Press, 1999), 40.
62. Soon, Brass, Heinze & Haynes, "Unconscious Determinants of Free Decisions in the Human Brain." *Nature Neuroscience*, April 13th, 2008. (as reported in www.exploringthemind.com/the-mind/brain-scans-can-reveal-your-decisions-7-seconds-before-you-decide).
63. McRaty, R., M. Atkinson, R.T. Bradley, "Electrophysiologial Evidende of Intutition: Part 1. The surprising Role of the Heart, *Journal of Alternative and Complementary Medicine* 2004; 10(1): 133-143.
64. Ji, Sayer, "Biophotons: The Human Body Emits, Communicates with, and is Made from Light." www.greenmedinfo.com/blog/biophotons-human-body-emits-communicates-and-made-light.
65. Chopra, Deepak, "The Law of Least Effort," *The Chopra Center.* www.chopra.com/community/online-library/the-seven-spiritual-laws-of-success/the-law-of-least-effort.
66. Cooper, Belle Beth, "What Happens to the Brain When You Meditate," lifehacker.com/what-happens-to-the-brain-when-you-meditate-and-how-it-1202533314.
67. Strogatz, Stephen *Sync: The Emerging Science of Spontaneous Order*, (New York: Hachette Books, 2003).
68. Wiswell, John. Review of Sync. Wiswell states, Synchrony is a science in its infancy, and Strogatz is a pioneer in this new frontier in which mathematicians and physicists attempt to pinpoint just how spontaneous order emerges from chaos. www.goodreads.com/book/show/354421.Sync
69. Banned TED Talk about Psychic Abilities: Russell Targ. This talk was originally slated as part of a TEDx event in 2013, but TED pulled their support when they learned about the subjects (psychic abilitites and remote viewing). In this video, Targ says "Everyone can quiet the mind and describe an experience at a distance. Looking into the distance is no harder than looking at something nearby: nonlocal connections." www.youtube.com/watch?v=hBl0cwyn5GY
70. Nierenberg, Cari, "The Science of Intuition, How to measure Hunches and Gut Feelings," *Live Science.* Accessed May 20, 2016: www.livescience.com/54825-scientists-measure-intuition.html.
71. Ibid.

72. To view, means practitioners within the field of Remote viewing use specific protocols that allow them to tap into information via inherent mental processes whereby they receive information from all other matter and energy.
73. The well-known "Stargate Project," which was declassified in April of 1995; it is the code name for several sub-projects established by the U.S. Federal Government.
74. Puthoff, Howard.E., "Toward a Quantum Theory of Life Process," Unpublished proposal, Stanford Research Institute (1972).
75. Documented in "Paraphysics R&D–Warsaw Pact (U)" DST-1810S-202-78, *Defense Intelligence Agency* (30 March 1978).
76. Puthoff, Harold E. and Targ, Russell, "Perceptual Augment Techniques" *SRI Progress Report No. 3,* (31 Oct. 1974), and Final Report (1 Dec. 1975) to the CIA.
77. Jahn, R.G.; B.J. Dunne (1986), "On the Quantum Mechanics of Consciousness with Application to Anomalous Phenomena," *Foundations of Physics* 18(6): 721-772.
78. Jahn, Robert G. (1982). "The Persistent Paradox of Psychic Phenomena: An Engineering Perspective," *Proceedings of the IEEE.* Volume 70: 136-170.
79. Henderson, Nicole Myers prior publications: "Cellular Memory and Cellular Memory Detoxification," Holos University Library determines that our sensory systems are fed information continuously from outside stimuli and the environment;See also "Rapture Beyond Quantum Consciousness," and "On Sacred Time Tapping the Power Within." (Mustang: Tate Publishing & Enterprises, 2014).
80. Schiffman, H.R., *Sensation and Perception, An Integrated Approach*, Third Edition, (New York: John Wiley & Sons, 1976, 1982, 1990), 452.
81. Loewenstein, Werner, *The Touchstone of Life*, (London: Oxford University Press, 1999).
82. Loewenstein, *The Touchstone of Life*, suggested microscopic books of DNA.
83. Walia, Arjun "Nothing is solid, everything is Energy," *Collective Evolution*; September 27, 2014: www.collective-evolution.com/2014/09/27/this-is-the-world-of-quantum-physics-nothing-is-solid-and-everything-is-energy/.
84. Franson, James, *Theory of Relativity*, University of Maryland. Thought is made from energy. Franson suggests that light travels at constant speed of 299,792,458 meters per second in a vacuum. Thought or Information is said to move faster than light, breaking

the light barrier and being random; often seen as useless (but can include future research into Quantum Entanglement and Negative Matter).

85. Anderson, Mark, "Is Quantum Mechanics Controlling Your Thoughts?," *Discover Magazine: Science for the Curious*. Accessed February 2009: discovermagazine.com/2009/feb/13-is-quantum-mechanics-controlling-your-thoughts.
86. Tanner, Lindsey, "Brain Waves are Window into Autism Language Woes," *The Mercury*, Dec. 1, 2008: www.pottsmerc.com/lifestyle/brain-waves-are-window-into-autism-language-woes/article_e8be4e4b-3d67-53f1-9fa6-b59ec120633c.html.
87. Swingle, Mairi, *iMinds*, Chapter 6, audiobook edition, (New Westminster: Posthypnotic Press Inc., 2016).
88. Hitt, Jack. "This is Your Brain on God." *Wired*, Accessed on July 11 1999: www.wired.com/wired/archive/7.11/persinger_pr.html.
89. Wikipedia Article: "Brain Activity and Medication," https://en.wikipedia.org/wiki/Brain_activity_and_meditation.
90. Editorial, "Theta Healing; Theta Brain State" *ThetaHealing*: www.thetahealing.com/about-thetahealing/thetahealing-theta-state.html.
91. "Brain Waves and Meditation," *Science Daily*, Accessed on March 31, 2010: www.sciencedaily.com/releases/2010/03/100319210631.htm
92. Swingle, Mairi, *iMinds*, Chapter 6, Posthypnotic Press Inc, 2016).
93. Ibid.

APPENDIX

Goodreads List of Books About Intuition, June 2016
(https://www.goodreads.com/shelf/show/intuition)

Blink: The Power of Thinking Without Thinking (Paperback), by Malcolm Gladwell — published 2005.

The Gift of Fear: Survival Signals That Protect Us from Violence (Paperback), by Gavin de Becker — published 1997.

Gut Feelings: The Intelligence of the Unconscious (Hardcover), by Gerd GigerenzerGerd Gigerenzer — published 2007.

Increasing Intuitional Intelligence: How the Awareness of Instinctual Gut Feelings Fosters Human Learning, Intuition, and Longevity, by Martha Char Love — published 2015.

Intuition: Knowing Beyond Logic (Paperback) by OshoOsho — published 2001.

Your Sixth Sense (Paperback) by Belleruth NaparstekBelleruth Naparstek — published 1998.

Developing Intuition: Practical Guidance for Daily Life (Paperback) by Shakti Gawain — published 1987.

Trust Your Vibes: Secret Tools for Six-Sensory Living (Paperback) by Sonia Choquette — published 2004.

Discover Your Psychic Type: Developing and Using Your Natural Intuition (Paperback), by Sherrie Dillard — published 2008.

The Invisible Gorilla: And Other Ways Our Intuitions Deceive Us (Hardcover), by Christopher Chabris — published 2010.

Practical Intuition (Paperback), by Laura Day — published 1996.

The Intuitive Way: A Guide to Living from Inner Wisdom (Paperback), by Penney Peirce — published 1997.

Living in the Light: A Guide to Personal and Planetary Transformation (Paperback), by Shakti Gawain — published 1985.

Dance First, Think Later: 618 Rules to Live By (Paperback), by Kathryn Petras — published 2011.

Strategic Intuition: The Creative Spark in Human Achievement (Hardcover), by William Duggan — published 2007.

Eureka! Understanding and Using the Power of Your Intuition (Paperback), by Anne Salisbury — published 2008.

Intuition Pumps And Other Tools for Thinking (Paperback), by Daniel C. Dennett — published 2013.

Power of Intuition (Audio), by Deepak Chopra — published 2001.

Heart of Tarot: An Intuitive Approach (Paperback), by Amber K — published 2002.

Practical Intuition: How to Harness the Power of Your Instinct and Make It Work for You (Hardcover), by Laura Day — published 1996.

The Highly Intuitive Child: A Guide to Understanding and Parenting Unusually Sensitive and Empathic Children (Paperback) by Catherine Crawford— published 2008.

Think Twice: Harnessing the Power of Counterintuition (Hardcover), by Michael J. Mauboussin — published 2009.

Trust Your Gut: How the Power of Intuition Can Grow Your Business (Hardcover), by Lynn A. Robinson — published 2006.

The Art of Empathy: A Complete Guide to Life's Most Essential Skill (Paperback), by Karla McLaren — published 2013.

Becoming An Empath (Audio CD), by Karla McLaren — published 2000.

When GOD Winks on Love: Let the Power of Coincidence Lead You to Love (Paperback), by Squire Rushnell — published 2003.

The Boy Who Saw True: The Time-Honoured Classic of the Paranormal (Paperback), by Cyril Scott (Editor) — published 1953.

Hare Brain, Tortoise Mind: How Intelligence Increases When You Think Less (Paperback), by Guy Claxton — published 1997.

Looking Beyond: How To Use Your Psychic Talent To Get What You Want (Paperback), by James Van Praagh — published 2003.

Spirited: Connect to the Guides All Around You (ebook), by Rebecca Rosen — published 2010.

Opening the Inner Eye: Explorations on the Practical Application of Intuition in Daily Life and Work (Paperback), by William H. Kautz — published 2003.

The Book of Secrets (Vigyan Bhairav Tantra), by OshoOsho — published 1974.

Loving your Life!: Explorations on loving your self and your life more wondrously using the power of mBIT, Positive Psychology & NLP (Kindle Edition), by Grant soosalu — published 2015.

Celtic Visions: Seership, Omens and Dreams of the Otherworld (Hardcover), by Caitlín MatthewsCaitlín Matthews — published 2012.

The Ecstasy of Surrender: 12 Surprising Ways Letting Go Can Empower Your Life (Hardcover), by Judith Orloff — published 2014.

Dr. Judith Orloff's Guide to Intuitive Healing: 5 Steps to Physical, Emotional, and Sexual Wellness (Paperback), by Judith Orloff — published 2000.

ABOUT THE AUTHORS

Dr. Anne Watson is a retired Canadian Special Education Professor, a writer, an artist, and the inventor of the EEG *neurofeedback for two* procedure known as Mind Phasing. Her "So, You Have to Go To Court!" (1986) was a best-seller, contributing to the genesis of Victims' Service Workers. She has two beautiful and accomplished adult children, and one beloved granddaughter. She is a snowbird who lives in Mexico when Canada gets too cold.

www.drannewatson-russell.com   awatruss@gmail.com

Nicole Henderson is a Health and Wellness consultant, Energy Communication specialist, a philanthropist, writer and artist. She does not dream of retiring. Helping people and animals as she paves the way for the future generations and staying active are her true loves in life. She lives near Charlotte North Carolina with her husband and two dogs.

www.earthessenceinc.com   nhendersonsc@gmail.com

www.ingramcontent.com/pod-product-compliance
Lightning Source LLC
Chambersburg PA
CBHW070043120526
44589CB00035B/2301